A WASP
AMONG
EAGLES

Ann Carl in her WASP uniform.

A WASP AMONG EAGLES

*A
Woman Military
Test Pilot
in World War II*

Ann B. Carl

SMITHSONIAN INSTITUTION PRESS

Washington and London

Copy editor: Initial Cap Editorial Services
Production editor: Ruth Spiegel
Designer: Martha Sewall

Library of Congress Cataloging-in-Publication Data
Carl, Ann B. (Baumgartner)
    A WASP among Eagles : a woman military test pilot in World War II / Ann B. Carl.
        p.   cm.
    Includes bibliographical references and index.
    ISBN 1-56098-842-8 (alk. paper)
    1. Carl, Ann Baumgartner   2. World War, 1939–1945—Aerial operations, American.
3. World War, 1939–1945—Personal narratives, American.   4. Women Airforce Service Pilots (U.S.)—Biography.   5. Women air pilots—United States—Biography.
6. Women test pilots—United States—Biography.   I. Title.
D790.C272   1999
940.54′4973′082—dc21   98-39772
                                                                                              CIP

British Library Cataloguing-in-Publication Data available

Manufactured in the United States of America
05 04 03 02 01 00 99   5 4 3 2 1

♾ ⊕ The recycled paper used in this publication meets the minimum requirements
of the American National Standard for Information Sciences—Permanence of Paper
for Printed Library Materials ANSI Z39.48-1984.

Contents

A winged steed, unwearying in flight,
Sweeping through the air swift as a gale of wind.
—HESIOD, The Catalogue of Women

DEDICATION AND ACKNOWLEDGMENTS

This book deals with a particular time in World War II history and involves real people, many of them well known, even famous. Realizing the grave responsibilities in presenting them in my narrative, I have described them as I knew them. What they say and do in this book is based on my recollection of day-to-day contact with them, on old letters, and on more recent conversations. And to them all, this book is dedicated.

My account of flight testing at a time when the speed of sound was a barrier to overcome on the way to greater speed of aircraft might never have been written without the impetus and encouragement of these people: Ethel Finley, president, WASP (Women Airforce Service Pilots), 1992–94; Dr. R. R. Gilruth of the NACA (later NASA); Maj. Kenneth Rowe, Administrator of Aviation (Ret.), Commonwealth of Virginia; John Tebbel, historian, and Col. Nathan Rosengarten, chief of Flight Research, Wright Field Air Force Base.

Along the way, NASA historian Deborah Douglas contributed discerning and helpful suggestions. And my editor and literary agent, William B. Goodman, always professional and tactful, kept me squarely on the road through dark valleys of discouragement and ephemeral highpoints. With expertise, Ruth Spiegel, production editor at the Smithsonian Institution Press, and copyeditor Therese Boyd prepared the book for publication.

My husband, Bill, besides being part of the story, suffered through my solitary throes of creation and then carefully (and kindly) checked my facts and helped clarify my technical explanations.

INTRODUCTION

During the 1990s controversy over whether or not women should fly military aircraft in combat, it was suddenly brought to light that 50 years earlier a thousand women were quietly flying Air Force military aircraft of all kinds. Their job had been to release men for combat in World War II while they, as it were, took care of home-port flying.

Oddly enough, the permission for combat granted to the 1990 women flyers became overshadowed by a frenzy for celebrating those forgotten ladies of the misty past of the 1940s. They had no publicity at the time. In fact, they had very little status. They served as Civil Service personnel "attached" to the Army Air Forces. It was not until 1977, thanks to Sen. Barry Goldwater among others, that legislation was finally passed making them full-fledged members of the Air Force.

These were the WASPs—Women Airforce Service Pilots. Without fanfare, they served in World War II from 1942 to 1945. In December 1944, the WASPs were disbanded, and, except among themselves, forgotten.

Already licensed pilots, they had been recruited by famous aviators Nancy Love and Jacqueline Cochran, who had persuaded Gen. H. H. "Hap" Arnold that experienced women pilots could take over flying jobs at home. About two dozen of the most experienced (with over 500 hours of flying time) were sent to England immediately to assist the women's Air Transport Auxiliary of the RAF. Another dozen were assigned to the U.S. Air Transport Command to ferry new aircraft then flowing from production lines to U.S. bases and export points. (Contrary to some reports, the WASPs did not fly bombers transatlantic to England.)

To keep the supply of women coming, Jackie Cochran organized a training program that followed exactly the Air Force cadet program of primary, basic, and advanced flight training and ground school. Even the training aircraft were the same. Although 25,000 women applied, only 1,800 were selected and of these only about 1,000 received their wings. Thirty-eight lost their lives while in service.

Women came from every kind of occupation—from bartender to physician, from journalist to actress—but all of them became capable, patriotic members of the Air Force flying community. And many had family members in service as well. These women flew every kind of Air Force plane. Most ferried planes to bases. Others towed targets for artillery gunners, some were instructors, some flew special planes. In fact, they flew, without regard to risk, whatever they were asked to fly. They did not, however, aspire to fly in combat overseas.

The years 1993–95 have been celebrated as the fiftieth anniversary of the WASPs. They have been sought out, individually and en masse, to speak and be on display. Uniforms have been brought out of mothballs and the stories of their wartime derring-do have at last been told.

I have a unique addendum to this story, and I have been urged by many people and organizations to set it down. Quite simply, as an experimental test pilot with the Air Force, I flew our first jet fighter and, in fact, became the first woman to fly a jet aircraft. That was in October 1944. I was on a special assignment to Wright-Patterson Air Force test center, where all experimental aircraft were rigorously evaluated before acceptance by the Air Force and where these aircraft were also tested against captured enemy aircraft. There was danger involved, and the pilots here were either seasoned combat pilots or aeronautical engineers, often both. They were head of the class of the Air Force, as Wright Field was the heart of the Air Force. To be assigned to work with these pilots was indeed a privilege.

Although I am basically more interested in writing about others (after the WASPs were disbanded, I joined the Wright Field public relations department to write news stories about the test-pilot heroes), I have been persuaded that it is important that this special and intriguing WASP tale be told. Therefore, in this short book, I have tried to explain (people have asked) how I happened to fly in the first place, what it was like to be on this separate assignment, and what it led to.

But mostly, this is about being the only woman test pilot at Wright Field during World War II and about being fortunate enough to be a pioneer in the jet age.

CHAPTER 1

Roots

"You have aids to help you now that we, of course, never had. You have strain gauges and barographs and wind tunnel tests, for example, to tell you what the forces are on various parts of the aircraft in different maneuvers. We made calculations and built our gliders and just tried them out. Sometimes it was very discouraging. As you know, we wrecked some of them before we learned what made them fly and especially what made them turn. And then we had to create an engine and try it."

It was Orville Wright speaking.

We were standing in front of the Fighter Flight Test hangar at the edge of the north-south runway of Wright Field Air Force Base in Dayton, Ohio. It was early 1944, during the period when our developing aircraft companies were trying to sell to the Air Force their faster fighter planes and longer range bombers for the pilots flying combat in World War II. Wright Air Force Base, where these new planes would be tested, incorporated Huffman Prairie, where the Wright brothers did much of their early testing. (Later it was to include neighboring Patterson Air Force Base to become the Wright-Patterson Air Force Base.)

"Test pilots today are really scientists," Wright continued. "Many are aeronautical engineers."

"It is still a hazardous career, though," I ventured. "They are pioneering into unknowns, the sound barrier, compressibility and other barriers. It's as dangerous for the neophyte test pilot, with lots to learn, as for the experts who are asked to push on beyond known boundaries. Don't you think so?"

"Yes, pioneering will always be dangerous."

Orville often came down, in his overcoat and hat, to our hangar to talk "aviation." And I felt honored to be included in these conversations. We stood in awe of this soft-spoken, pleasant man. Think of the barriers to flight he and Wilbur broke through! And yet here he was, still probing the new problems and developments of flight. He especially wanted to talk about jet propulsion with Fighter Test chiefs Maj. Fred Borsodi and Maj. Gus Lundquist. So far, we had not seen the secret jet fighter, the Bell XP-59A, but there were rumors that one of these experimental jets was coming to Wright Field for evaluation.

We watched a P-51 land on the runway and taxi back to the hangar, its engine popping and spitting. The pilot was Major Borsodi, returning from compressibility dive tests on the plane. Orville had been waiting for him.

"I'm fascinated by the jet. What a simple means of propulsion. How we worked and reworked our first little pusher engine. Aviation will soar ahead, though its progress between our 1903 flight and today still takes my breath away. Women even fly military planes now!"

The P-51 came to a stop, its propeller slowly stopped turning, and the engine gave a final backfire. Borsodi pushed back the cockpit canopy and climbed out on the wing. Orville turned back to me for a moment.

"You must fly that jet. I'll be rooting for you. And how I'd love to fly it, too. But I'm close to 80 years old, you know." (Though Wilbur, four years the elder, had died in 1912 at the age of 45, Orville would live until 1948 and age 77.)

"I certainly hope I can," I said.

"But what kind of a girl would want to fly an experimental jet? A pioneer like me, maybe!"

"Not quite like you. You started it all. You were the first men to create and fly a vehicle that was truly an air-craft."

Yet this kindly man had taken a moment to encourage an eager young flyer. But could I, even to myself, answer his question? Indeed, what kind of a "girl" was I?

Looking back 50 years to the exciting and well-remembered days of WASP flying during World War II is easy compared to the test which Orville Wright put to me—to start way back at the beginning to explain what sort of individual I had become by the time of that flying.

To define a person—any person—is a daunting task. It goes so far beyond the outer shell—of how a person looks, walks, dresses, talks, gestures. Inside the person is a self that encompasses more than the world he lives in. It is nearly impossible to guess *correctly* what profession a person is in, with no helpful hints.

And knowing the profession is only the starting point. Of course one needs to know why that profession was chosen, what problems he or she had to solve, what disappointments met, what victories won. All that, too, is mere curriculum vitae material. What about the deeper, more elusive world? What are the person's dreams? And what sets them off—music, pictures, conversations, books, scents, wine?

And the moods—one day buoyant, the next uncertain. The Chaos scientists say one butterfly in the air above California affects the whole nation's weather. Just so, unsuspected influences mysteriously affect people and remain in the psyche, things like a disappointing vacation, a day the rain spoiled a dress, an exhilarating mountain view, a thrilling symphony concert.

As important, of course, are the outside influences of the very era in which the person lives, his historical milieu. But must we know a person's medical history, ancestry, and genetic makeup? We know no two selves are the same— though sometimes two may seem endearingly similar. Some selves stretch as far as interstellar space, even venture into unknowns, while others simply stagnate and venture nowhere.

In any case, catching the whole person, the real self, is to reach for the ephemeral.

When the self to be described is your own self, the telling becomes a combination of true confession and police report. One must stand outside and look, unflinchingly, inside.

I was a war baby, born in August 1918 in an army hospital in Augusta, Georgia, while my father was fighting in the Amiens region of France. And I went from the hospital where I had been carried about by the nurses to smile and gurgle to entertain the wounded soldiers, to my father's parents' house on the New Jersey coast to await his return. There I annoyed my new grandparents with my crying.

"In all my four boys, I never had a baby who cried like that one," my poor mother was told. She used to sit on the stairs at night, she told me, to try to rock me to sleep. (I don't know that I ever made up for that.)

But after the Armistice in France, and my father's return, we moved to a small shingled bungalow in Plainfield, New Jersey, where we would be within commuting distance of New York City.

My parents were married shortly after my father was taken into the U.S. Army. They had met in New York City where my father was a beginning lawyer in Kenyon and Kenyon, a patent law firm in New York and Washington, D.C. My mother was studying art at the Parsons School of Art and Design and doing small design jobs. They were living in the same boarding house on the Upper West Side. When my father left for his first training camp, my mother followed and caught up with him in Davenport, Iowa, where they were married. They had only a short overnight visit to Halifax, Nova Scotia, for a honeymoon.

The bungalow was their first home together. It stood between a tall, forbidding Victorian house and a rather rundown house that was nearly hidden by large trees. But I remember my mother's garden, where the flowers were as tall as I was and where interesting buzzing insects and butterflies lived.

A horse and wagon delivered milk each day, and sometimes I was boosted up aboard the horse for a short ride. Most every day my mother took me along on visits to her friends' art studios. While they talked about benefit art exhibits, I wandered about, noting the sunbeams in the shafts of light from the windows and playing with the resident cats. One day out of boredom, I guess, I followed a group of jolly older children walking by and was later returned home via the police. Though my father took an early train to New York and a late one home at night, on weekends he spent time with me and showed me how all the mechanical things worked. When I was covered with chicken pox, he got down on the floor and played games with me, like rolling toy trucks back and forth.

When I was 4, my brother Tom was born. We moved to a larger house so Tom could have a room of his own, and the next year I started school. I liked helping my mother take care of small Tommy, and later got good marks for pulling him back from the middle of the road where he had pushed his kiddie car. But, more often, I was called down for being selfish, for not considering other people, for chattering too much about myself. This reprimand carried over to later life, where I thought twice before "chattering on about myself." (Still do.)

We lived right across the street from the square, brick Evergreen Public School. My mother usually walked with me to school and stopped to chat with the class teacher. There were about 20 students in each class. They came from the immediate neighborhood as well as outlying areas. Certain students still stand out, as well as the tall windows in the room, the smell of chalk, and the sound of it on the blackboard.

I remember Bergen Van Arsdale, whose father ran a large men's clothing store, and Herbert Stine, a whiz at arithmetic. Always in the back row was Thomas Day, a quiet black boy (called "colored" then), who produced beautiful drawings. Then there was another Ann, a girl who, people said, lived in the woods. Her clothes were dirty, her hair unkempt, and she even smelled. She would never talk to us, and always seemed frightened. We were too young to imagine what her home life must have been like. Another girl, Josephine Viviano, had a brother who was a famous football star at Notre Dame.

All in all, Evergreen School was enjoyable. I liked learning new things and trying out new skills like reading, writing, and drawing. Herbert Stine and I skipped the second grade, and I won a citywide school poster contest on "keeping your city clean." (I always suspected that I'd won because my mother knew the teachers so well.)

My mother was quite active in our Episcopal church. She took me with her on Sundays, and I began to learn hymns and prayers and the idea of God. I also "helped" her take care of the altar before and after services, when the church was quiet and shadowy and, I thought, felt like a "house of God."

For my six-year-old Christmas, my parents made me a wonderful big doll-house, with electric lights, antique furniture, and a front panel that came off for play. I enjoyed it when friends came to play, but when I played with it by myself I had the strange thought that some unseen beings might be playing with me, just as I was playing with the dolls in the dollhouse. (Now, a grand-child is enjoying it, as far as I know, with no such thoughts.)

Things changed after we got to know our neighbors well and their two children played with us. The children went to private schools, so I was entered in Miss Hartridge's School for Girls, and Marion, the neighbor girl, and I walked to school each day. I was embarrassed to walk past my old school-mates (and they razzed me, too). Transferring to Hartridge, I skipped another grade to be in Marion's grade, the sixth grade. On top of that, I won an essay contest, and teachers began to treat me somewhat specially.

All this ostracized me from the sixth-grade clique of girls. I began to asso-ciate good school performance with the loss of friends. My response was to be defiant—one day, for instance, I simply stepped out the open low window in history class, and, of course, later had to discuss this and other uncooperative acts with Miss Hartridge, a large and formidable lady.

Another thing that aroused my classmates' derision was my Scottish attire, kilts, high socks, white blouse, and Scottish wool sweater. "Well, you have a perfect right to wear the Stuart kilt," my mother would say.

Out would come her family tree, and there the line could be followed (some-what circuitously) back to Mary Queen of Scots, and from there to Margaret Bruce, daughter of Robert the Bruce. Among less remote (1800 rather than 1300) forebears there was Sir Thomas Dundas, who is alleged to have rescued the parents of Queen Victoria from France so that Victoria would be born in England and thus become queen. He was made an earl thereby, but actually all he did was pay their debts—no thrilling midnight escape in a small boat and rough passage across the English Channel—yet it did make a difference in the history of the British throne. More recently (1900 and on), there were gener-als and admirals. One, Lord Zetland, was Viceroy to India. Another, Sir Ver-non Kell, started the "spy" agency MI-5. Another, Saury Gilpin, was a famous "sporting" artist.

The most recent "cousin," however, is Sir Hugh Dundas, RAF fighter Ace in World War II. And, interestingly enough, he, like me, turned to newspaper work after the war. We have corresponded, but not met.

They were a colorful, active lot, yet now, after two world wars, the family is decimated by the loss of its men.

The British, my mother impressed upon me, are reticent about themselves, do not discuss "money" and worth, but do value culture—art, music, books—and cherish their land and gardens, their countryside, pageantry, and history.

The family lived near the Scottish border, in Yorkshire. There is still a family castle in Skelton, dating from 1100, where we have often stayed. The story goes that on the eve of a death, a coach and four can be heard rattling across the bridge over the moat but never seen. Although I feel close to these forebears and my values are akin to theirs, who can say whether this is because of common genes or simply exposure.

My mother was actually just half-British, through her father, Charles Gilpin-Brown. Her mother, Helen Graham Poland, was a Bostonian. My grandparents met in Colorado in the late 1800s, when Helen's father moved his large family to Colorado because doctors said he needed the high altitude and clear air. He knew nothing about ranching. He ran the Poland Spring-Water Company and sailed a large sloop out of Nahant. But he planned to homestead in the lands west of Fort Collins.

These wild lands of mesquite and prairie grass in the foothills of the Rockies were just opening to homesteading. There was nothing to soften the harshness and dangers to anyone unused to the wilderness. The Polands might well have succumbed to this rigorous life had they not met two brothers establishing a ranch on neighboring land. They, too, were homesteading.

From Yorkshire, England, the Gilpin-Brown brothers were the youngest of several brothers and thus, following British custom, were not in line to inherit family land or become naval or army officers, or even churchmen. But they had always lived on the land in England, and kindly assisted the Poland family in establishing their ranch and purchasing their cattle and horses. Later, my grandmother married one of the brothers, Charles Gilpin-Brown. They then established their own ranch and had two daughters, Margaret (my mother) and Frances.

My father, viewing my mother's grandiose British genealogical picture with some skepticism, liked to say that *his* important Swiss ancestor was the fellow called Baumgartner who rowed the patriot William Tell across Lake Lucerne, where he had been sentenced to shoot an apple off his son's head during the Swiss struggle for freedom. It must have been because of that, my father said, that he had always liked to row a boat! He rowed on the college rowing team at Lehigh University, where he was an engineering student, and rowed on the Potomac River when he was studying law at Georgetown University in Washington, D.C.

(Incidentally, Baumgartner is a very common name in Switzerland, but it was the source of humor for my schoolmates who liked to call me "Bum garter" or "Rotten elastic." Later, flying schedules posted on the bulletin board listed me as "Baum+." At Wright Field, I was simply Ann to all.)

My father's family had been in the United States for five generations, living in Trenton, New Jersey, across from another engineer, John Roebling, the great bridge designer. Besides his parents, my father had three brothers, all of whom became engineers, though one would have studied medicine if his father had not forbidden it. But the Swiss must be more reticent than the Brits because their only told and retóld family story was about a murder at their house while the family was in church. A boyfriend shot the cook dead in the dining room. Darkened newspaper clippings, with gory pictures, still survive.

Plainfield, in the years between the world wars and before the Great Depression during the 1930s, like most American towns then, was a peaceful, safe place to live. The shocking news of the day was only about embezzlements at banks or the rare midnight robbery of a pharmacy, or stories of the odd town drunk. Movies were fit for the most naive child, policemen were considered honorable, conscientious men. It was a time of patriotism, of consideration of others—a truly Norman Rockwell era.

Though our mothers, in telling us about marriage and sex, included warnings of "white slavery" operations, it was still safe for small girls to explore the woods and city streets. My friends and I, on our bikes, even visited falling-down abandoned houses and tried to figure out why the people had left. Young boys and girls stayed just boys and girls until well into the teens.

While my brother learned how to tie nautical knots in the Cub Scouts, I took ballet and piano lessons at Miss Ransome's School of the Dance. Oddly enough, this early dancing had an effect, later, on my flying. Instructors noticed that my coordination, especially from one maneuver to another, seemed smoother than most students'. Ballet had apparently taught me balance and a sense of the whole aircraft around me. Another by-product of the ballet school was a supply of costumes which found second life in dressing neighbor children in small plays I wrote and charged neighbors 10 cents to watch.

I remember that the weather then was much colder than it has been of late. There was deep snow most of the winter. The town trucks plowed night and day. We took our Flexible Flyer sleds to slide down the golf course hills. The roads were so icy at night that people brought out ancient sleighs drawn by horses trimmed with bells. As we lay in bed, we could hear the bells, the trotting hooves, and the hum of the runners on the ice. How I wished I was out there, too.

We both had small radios, called crystal sets, that my father made for us. We listened with earphones to classical music "coming out of the air." My father explained how the radio worked to my brother, and I felt left out. I was no longer the recipient of this sort of information.

Tom was more easygoing and conciliatory than I, but not as eager a student. We were always good friends, however. Later, he invited me up to a Cornell weekend as a blind date for a friend (and not as a joke). Service in the U.S. Marine Corps in 1944–45 interrupted his engineering studies, but he returned and earned his degree in engineering management. He also married a fellow student, Gabrielle Landt, an artist. He liked the Big Band sound and had many Glenn Miller records. His favorite was "Moonlight Serenade." I cannot hear it now without tears. Tom has since died of cancer.

We were a bit in awe of our father in our early years. Though he spent time with us and loved us, built us a big sandbox and a playhouse that had a front porch and windows on both sides, he could be very austere. Perhaps that is a good thing in a father, but he seemed very strict to us. My mother explained that his Presbyterian upbringing *had* been strict. He was strict with himself, leaning on such credos as "Only results count, merely trying is not enough." This, as my mother pointed out, was merely super-conscientiousness, after all. For example, if you were asked to weed the brick walk, you went ahead, even if the sun was hot and the others had gone for a swim, and you worked until the job was well done (tired, and dusty, and with skinned knuckles perhaps).

Yet, my mother, though she understood, was always careful to test the wind, so to speak. And I followed suit, when I had to relate some transgression or ask for a permission. In later years, I was still hesitant to put forth what I would like to do.

In 1928, when I was 10 and my brother 6, we spent a month on a cattle ranch in Colorado. The occasion was a reunion of the American members of the Poland and Gilpin-Brown families. For me it was a turning point. It was a time of maturation, of learning to take responsibility, of conquering fear. I learned I had to make decisions on my own. Certainly without realizing it, I was preparing the early groundwork necessary for future things like test flying.

CHAPTER 2

Awakenings

The ranch belonged to my grandmother's younger sister Ethel and her husband Gordon Johnson, and was in the same Rocky Mountain foothills northwest of Fort Collins where my grandmother's ranch had been. There were about two dozen of us: seven from my grandmother's generation, five from my mother's, eight older teens and three small (Tom, me, and cousin Sidney, 6).

The old ones slept in the ranch house. All the boys lived in a big white tent with a wooden floor. The girls slept in the open attic of the house. It was a new experience to live closely with so many, with so many different ages, all relatives. I was particularly in awe of the three girls sharing the attic with me. Their girl-talk enlightened me about all kinds of secrets older girls had. One of the girls had had cerebral palsy from birth, and often suffered spasms and loss of control. These we learned to treat simply with quiet patience. All of us were pretty fascinated by the high-spirited lads in the big white tent.

We traveled across the country by train, my mother, Tom, and I, and my grandmother and Aunt Fan, and met the others at the ranch. My grandmother was at that time dean of women at Columbia University Graduate School in New York City and Aunt Fan was an opera singer. My father would only be able to join us for the last week. Grandmother's husband had died on their ranch long before.

My grandmother, who had always told us exciting stories of her ranch life, now wanted us to hear what her trip west with her father in the late 1800s had been like. We were finding that sleeping aboard the train and struggling through the cars to the dining car was exciting enough. But as we sped through fields of nine-foot-tall corn in the Midwest she said to keep looking ahead.

"Before you know it," she said in her storytelling voice, "you will see the snowy peaks of mountains on the horizon. These are the Rocky Mountains, and when you see them, you'll know that Colorado is not too far away."

And sure enough, suddenly we saw them.

After we changed trains in Denver for Fort Collins farther north, she dropped her voice and said, "Long ago when we were on this train, Indians galloped along beside the train on their fast ponies and shot arrows into the cars. We had to get down on the floor so we wouldn't get hit." When she saw us looking around for Indians, she added, "The Indians don't do that now."

When we stopped for the night in Fort Collins, she said Fort Collins was a small cattle town in the 1800s, that herds of cattle were driven from Texas north to Wyoming, right through the town. "When I awoke in the morning, I could hear the lowing of cattle and the shouts of the Mexican cowboys driving the cattle through. I looked out the window and saw that the cattle spread as far as I could see," she said.

We, on the other hand, were met at the train by Uncle Gordon and driven in his old car over rough and muddy roads through the wild foothills of the Rockies to the ranch. Along the road into the ranch, we had several barbed-wire gates to undo and fasten up again (handling these gates is an art), and had to ford three rivers. My grandmother said to look for wild animals off the road under the trees—even for mountain lions.

"When your mother and Aunt Fan were little girls," she told us, "they were driving their little cart pulled by Jerry, their pony, along this very road when they saw a brown animal lying under a tree back from the road. They stopped Jerry as they thought it might be a sick cow. They didn't know what they should do, but decided to leave the cart and have a closer look. As they walked toward it, they saw it move its tail. Then it raised its head, and they saw it was not a cow but a mountain lion. Slowly, slowly, so not to arouse the lion, they turned and walked back to the cart, and they had Jerry walk slowly away. But can you imagine what might have happened if Jerry had caught the lion's scent when they left the cart, and run away?"

The log ranch house sat in a valley along the Cache la Poudre River. This was a working ranch, not a dude ranch. Though the main cattle were far away on the range, there were outbuildings and corrals, milk cows and riding horses near the house. The Cache la Poudre River rushed through the valley with its store of husky brown and rainbow trout. Each summer evening, angry thunderclouds bowled along its course, dragging veils of showers across the hills.

With so many persons living at the ranch, each one was assigned a job. The men ran the ranch, caught the fish, and killed and dressed the chickens. The women cooked and washed all the clothes in big steaming tubs and hung the laundry to dry in the wind. The girls tidied up, and set and cleared the long ranch dining-room table. All this work was accompanied by loud and happy singing of opera arias or favorite hymns. My grandmother and her brother (my great-uncle) Joe quoted by heart from Shakespeare or the Bible. This was how people entertained themselves on lonely ranches at that time.

I cannot remember what jobs my six-year-old brother and cousin Sidney had, but my special assignment was to ride out (after I learned to ride Comrade, the old black cowpony) to find and bring in the milk cows each evening.

When I first arrived at the ranch, I was rather a "scaredy" kid and a worrier. I did not join in, say, climbing trees until I had watched for a while, and I was not exactly keen on new adventures. I had to analyze things before I tried them. Of course, this rather annoying trait could be helpful when it came to testing planes much later.

So it was not surprising that one evening, when the daily thunderstorm came earlier than usual, I continued to sit on the porch and watch the grandeur of it rather than go for the cows at the appointed time.

Uncle Gordon suddenly appeared before me and asked, "Where are the milk cows?"

I looked up at my white-haired, stocky, weathered uncle and said, "Well, there's a thunderstorm."

"Why, they still must be brought in to be milked," Uncle Gordon answered.

Ashamed, I walked through the rain to the corral, brought Comrade in and saddled him up with my small Western saddle. Outside, the thunder rolled through and rain lashed the stable. As I tightened the cinch, Comrade turned and touched my arm with his nose. I patted him in return, and we started off into the storm.

Under the pelting rain, we climbed the rocky hill above the ranch house. From time to time, lightning bolts struck the rocks nearby, followed by sharp cracks of thunder. As Comrade picked his way along the path without flinching, I hunched over in the rain and turned up my collar to shut out the noise of the thunder and the driving rain. Small animals scurried across our path, and bushes leaned and whipped under the weight of the wind and the rain. Suddenly a quick movement drew our attention to a coiling snake. Then we heard the rattles. Comrade quickly trotted out of its way, then quietly resumed his steady pace. He had not been afraid; it was old hat to him. I patted him to thank him.

Our path became a rivulet, but as we sloshed along we did not find the cows at any of their usual stopping places. They could be anywhere in their miles-square pasture. We stopped to look around from a high point. At the top of one hill I saw a group of animals, but their profile was elliptical, not square, which meant, Uncle Gordon had told me, that they were horses, not cows.

Slipping and sliding, we went down in the valley to look. They were not there. We continued to look from higher ground, into gullies and cul-de-sacs.

It began to grow dark. At last, far from home, we saw them huddled together in a deep gully.

Comrade, the seasoned cowpony, went straight in, pushing the cows into line. There were about a dozen of them. However, they did not want to leave their safe refuge. Old Sookie, the lead cow—she was dun-colored and had a collar and a bell that was supposed to help tell where she was—blocked the way out. She stood shaking her head and horns at us and braced her legs in a halt. I ineffectually raised my quirt at her and yelled at her to move. But Comrade pushed her and forced her out. The others tagged along. Once on the way, with Comrade pushing Sookie on, we headed home.

As we descended our final hill, it was nearly dark but the storm had quieted considerably. We urged the herd into the corral and I closed them in. I removed Comrade's tack and rubbed him down. His drenched body was cold to the touch. I realized, back there at the age of 10, that Comrade had shown me what my father had tried to tell us—that you don't give up when things get hard, even dangerous, until you have finished your job, particularly when others are depending on you.

I had thought, I admit, that perhaps the family would be worried about us out in the storm so late and all. But they had nearly finished dinner when we came in.

Later, I heard my grandmother calling down Uncle Gordon. "You shouldn't have sent that child out in that storm."

"No, she's simply got to learn that when she has a job to do, it is her responsibility to do it."

Uncle Gordon was right. I did learn something from going out alone in the raging storm and completing my job of bringing in the cows who had to be milked each night. I hadn't run back in when I could not find them right away and, even with night coming on, I kept on. Now I even look back on the stinging rain, the vicious lightning and thunder, and the gathering darkness out in the wild pastureland with something approaching pleasure. I had conquered them—albeit with Comrade's help and example. I had taken a big step forward, from a habit of timidity to one of more mature achievement. It was a turning point. I was ready to tackle bigger challenges, and alone.

I had tasted the excitement and temptation of danger, and I liked it.

But life at the ranch was not all work. We hiked in the hills, taking picnic makings with us. Because we were over 6,000 feet in altitude, we were to keep ourselves in check when climbing. If we went too fast, our elders told us, we might get nosebleeds or maybe faint. We picnicked beside fast-running brooks, wading and slipping on the rocks. And we saw small herds of antelope run lightly ahead of us and into the cottonwood and aspen woods, and saw eagles dip into the river for fish. We did see mountain lion—at a distance—and we heard the eerie calls of coyotes at night.

Sometimes we rode out on the horses, riding back down the ranch road for eight miles to Livermore to pick up the mail. This meant dismounting to undo those wire gates and refastening them to keep grazing cattle and horses in. Sometimes the boys drove us up to Wyoming to see a rodeo. We girls would pick out favorite cowboy riders and giggle about them. There were square dances, too. I had fantasized about what dress I would wear and whom I would dance with, but only the older ones attended. My mother went, and my Aunt Fan, as well as my three roommates. I noticed how much younger my mother looked back out in Colorado, and how much fun she seemed to be having.

I could usually find an hour to steal away by myself on Comrade. I discovered the joy of exploring alone on the back of a horse, where the horse, in his responses to nature around him, acted as liaison for me into his natural world.

If we should meet an antelope, for instance, both Comrade and the antelope would stand motionless and gaze at one another until, finally, they apparently decided to trust one another and each would go his way. A lone crow, high in a tree, would give a single warning call to announce to the woods that we were coming. In the evening, an owl might pass us, at just horse-head level, without making a sound, more like a moving shadow than a bird.

Yet living on a Colorado cattle ranch, and making it go, is not easy. And it was a lot harder back in the late 1800s when my grandmother and her sisters and brothers had come out to homestead. First, there were unfriendly Indians about, as well as unfriendly terrain. Although household goods and utensils had been brought from Boston, tools, lumber, fencing, and, most important, horses and cattle had to be purchased, and from people not known. How would a Bostonian know what horses were good for a team to do work, for instance? And he wouldn't know how to work or train a team.

So it went. Much depended upon a family's relationship with local people and on its own self-reliance, ingenuity, and perseverance. The Polands were fortunate to have assistance from the Gilpin-Brown brothers. They saw many around them give up and go back east.

When my grandmother and Charles Gilpin-Brown started their ranch, Fort Collins and Livermore were established, though small, cattle towns. Ranchers knew and respected one another and joined together to accomplish the important yearly tasks, like driving the cattle down from the range and for inoculations and branding. My grandmother fed forty-odd cowboys three squares during the branding operation, and she was able to stitch up horses or cows who had tears in their skin from the wire fences. She was considered to be very pretty and very popular and was thought to be quite a catch when she was young.

Because of her Boston education, she felt a need to open a small school for the ranch children and for any Indian child who would come. When her husband died—when he was only 40 years old—she went to Greeley, Colorado, to teach at the state university. Then, in the early 1900s she took her two daughters back east to New York City where she became dean at Columbia University. Frances became a singer in the Metropolitan Opera, and my mother became an artist. But this grandmother, who had gone from "proper Bostonian" to ranch woman to widow to teacher and organizer of schools, and then moved east to become a university dean (and later dean at Katharine Gibbs School), would always be a role model for me.

I returned from the West more confident and more knowledgeable in many ways, not the least of which was what older girls do (whisper and giggle) and what they talk about (boys and their looks).

In 1929 came the stock-market crash, followed by the Depression years. Life became subdued and worrisome. Though my brother and I were too young to understand what was wrong, we noticed the many telephone calls from our father in New York and the serious discussions at home that included the word "bank." We had visitors, too, men who came to the back door looking for work, any kind; some even asked for food. It was a case of those who could helping those who were less fortunate.

When things settled down a bit, I was sent off for the summer to Camp Mudjekeewis ("West Wind"), a girl's camp on Lake Kezar in Maine. Here there was a different sort of exploring and adventure.

I went with older girls on long, three-week group canoe trips. We had three in a canoe, plus supplies and bedrolls. We wandered down the Saco River, often carrying the canoe overland between river and lakes. We traded off paddling positions each hour, the most tiring being the bow position. At night, we camped at farms where we could purchase eggs and milk. Often in the morning we awoke to find a curious cow standing over us. Later I went with my family on trips along the much wilder Alligash River in northern Maine.

The camp certainly took advantage of being on a lake. Before breakfast we had to jump in when the ground fog still lay on the water. After breakfast we put our wet and sandy bathing suits back on for lessons. These included lifesaving, where a large counselor grabbed you in an overpowering embrace—under water—and you had to break the hold and swim her safely to shore. In the late afternoon, in wet bathing suits again, we had a free (but compulsory) swim time. Often, however, Rudy Vallee (a popular singer of the time), who lived across the lake, circled about in his flashy mahogany speedboat—to the accompaniment of squeals from the girls.

There were other camp trips. Some included horseback riding. On others, we climbed the peaks of the Presidential Range, including Mount Washington, the East's highest mountain.

Mudjekeewis was also a music camp. The three directors played piano, violin, and cello as a trio, and we sang each night, as well as grace at each meal. The cellist had known my Aunt Fan in New York when she was singing at Town Hall Club and with the Met. She did not know, however, that the Met had given my aunt a choice (an ultimatum, in fact). Either she gave up smoking or lost her place at the Met (as ingenue singer). Sadly, she would not or could not give up smoking. (Now we know that nicotine is addictive.)

When I was about 14, my parents decided to move to the country. They first tried Wilton, Connecticut, renting a house suggested to us by the parents of a friend I had at Mudjekeewis. This semirestored colonial farmhouse, situated among tall elm trees atop Nod Hill, belonged to a New York editor. He had converted a small, vine-covered outbuilding into his library. Books lined every wall, sat in piles on the floor, were tucked into the shelves everywhere. I spent glorious afternoons here, picking and choosing books of all descriptions. I even slept here sometimes.

But Connecticut was not as handy to lower New York City as New Jersey was, and in the end we moved near Bernardsville, New Jersey. There was a barn there, and soon there were two horses in it. Mine was a tall, placid, chestnut thoroughbred, who was subjected to six o'clock in the morning "training" sessions. He was learning to jump and I was learning the English hunting seat. When the lessons went well, we wandered out afterward through the countryside, sometimes with my mother on her mare, and enjoyed the broad high fields and the denizens who lived in the woods and grass.

Later I exchanged him for a rather flashy chestnut mare that not everyone could ride. (To ride difficult horses was a conceit then.) Her performance in the hunting field was exemplary and led to my training other people's hunters and to painting horse portraits.

To improve my drawing, I took a summer course with George Bridgeman at Art Student's League in New York. My first day there I dashed off a quick drawing of our nude model, with a few horse sketches around the side (to show off). Mr. Bridgeman was passing from student to student, critiquing each drawing. When he got to me he stopped and asked, "Well, are you all through? Where are the muscles, and the bones in this model? The form?"

He made a few dark, basic lines.

"Work on this. What do your eyes tell you? We spend hours on one drawing here. And analysis would help your horses, too."

And he went on to the next student, as I turned very red. I looked over at the other student drawings. They all looked like Michelangelo compared to mine. It was not until I had managed to do a decent study of the model that I allowed myself to get an ice-cream cone to eat on the train going back to New Jersey. There weren't many ice-cream-cone days.

About this time, my father was active in the development of television. One morning, my mother and I were asked to take part in an experiment in New York. While I stayed in a downtown office in which a screen similar to a home movie screen was set up, Mother went to a similar office uptown. We were to test TV communication. Though her image was a bit watery, I could see it was she and heard her voice, and she heard mine. We were TV pioneers!

In the late 1930s, I attended Walnut Hill School in Natick, Massachusetts (a friend of my mother's in art school had advised it). It was not one of the "social" schools, where one learned the proper accent, the proper kind of sweater, and who was who in society. Rather, the school sought girls interested in college and in becoming good citizens, but also girls with extracurricular interests—a tennis player, a violin student, scientific collectors, painters, girls who wrote stories or poetry. In fact, today, the school (now coed), besides training for college, emphasizes the arts. Graduates go on to music conservatories, theater groups, and publications, and work toward becoming well-known professionals in their field.

On my own, away from home and among stimulating and supportive people, I was learning to be a person, learning to stand on my own two feet. There were new stiff courses—lab courses for the first time, four years of Latin, four years of French, literature and writing, and extensive history. This was the classical education good schools offered at that time. There was no softening of standards, no basket-weaving or flower-arranging courses then. In addition, there were athletics—field hockey, soccer, tennis, riding, skiing in the winter—and after classes, art and music. We fit in a theatrical production or two each year as well.

And I was interested in all of it.

One week, I imagined myself a great artist and studied Leonardo da Vinci's notebooks. The next, I examined the lives of great writers or became a world traveler speaking many languages or performing miracles as a great physician. This was to be a lifelong problem—my interest in too many activities at the same time. But many interesting doors to life seemed to be opening then.

One day, Miss Daniels, the school dean, asked me to come into her office. We sat down in her shadowy room.

"We've been looking over your marks, and you will be graduating with honors. Therefore, you will be excused from most of the College Board Exams. Well, aren't you pleased?"

I was not particularly pleased, and I guess it showed. I recalled my Hartridge School experience, and decided not to tell anyone, though Walnut Hill girls wouldn't have cared and there were others with honors as well. But my father often said girls shouldn't be smart, and if they were (especially scientific ones) would probably never get married. It was a "woman's place is in the home" era. I feared my father might be right, because I had no real boyfriend until I was in college. Not that I actually wanted one, because girls in that time and at that age (15, 16) were still happy doing girl things—still striving to excel on the tennis court, the art exhibit, or skiing, for example. Some played bridge endlessly.

We talked about sex, but it didn't shout at us from every facet of life as it does today. We weren't continuously being challenged to be "sexy" or to favor products with sexy advertisements. We still thought in terms of romantic love, the way our mothers had described it when relating the facts of life to us. And those revelations had been rather hazy, too. No one talked about sexual aberrations or excesses. They weren't front-page news then. Only in literature did we find (surreptitiously) such things as incest, sexual abuse, or even prostitution.

Although I remember certain courses and teachers well—the French history class where we spoke and took notes only in French, ancient history taught by a fledgling archaeologist, art and English where no imaginative idea was squelched—the one that was to affect my later choices most was Miss Ellis's science class.

Miss Ellis, of medium age and medium height, had short cropped curly grey hair, pink cheeks, and steady blue eyes that turned steely when confronted with some poor excuse for not knowing proper answers or not doing work. An early Carl Sagan, she made science come alive. In the lab, she had us watch carefully as the wonder of chemical changes took place. In lectures she carried us from the mysterious workings of weather farther into the heavens for a look at the stars and planets and nebulae. She introduced us to the microscope and the teeming life in a drop of water. Yet she never singled out individual students with advice to pursue science. It was a case of "This is science. Take it or leave it." But she did leave us with an Ovid quotation: "God gave man an upright countenance to survey the heavens, and to look upward to the stars."

Most of the Walnut Hill girls went on to New England girls' colleges. And here they changed from "girls" to "young women." Two of us had chosen Smith College in Northampton, Massachusetts, for its purportedly good art course and entered in the Class of 1939. But I, after arriving there and studying the courses suggested for freshmen, chose zoology and advanced chemistry: science instead of art courses. Because of Miss Ellis's introduction to science and all its intricacies and my good marks in it, I thought, if I could do it, a career in science would be more worthwhile, that I could contribute more. My major would be pre-med.

Nevertheless, I soon found that most of the other women had also been at the top of their high school classes, so competition would be greater. These women were more diverse than Walnut Hill students as well. Many were on scholarships. (These, I decided later, applied themselves and got more out of college than some of the rest of us who wasted time, but were supposedly "more fortunate.")

And there was quite a big percentage of foreign students. One of my best friends had come from China, another from Spain. There were a few young black women, but race was not only not in contention then but there was no thought of or plans for "affirmative action." It was an innocent time.

Most of us lived in three-story, vine-covered, old brick houses standing in a line along the main street, although, across the campus there were new, modern (characterless, we thought) quadrangles. My house, Tyler, last in the "old" line, was at the top of a hill that led down to a lake, and was across from Seelye, the music building, and the gymnasium, where the Modern Dance Group met. Behind our house were the Playhouse and the zoology building, Burton Hall. The other building important to my courses, the chemistry building, was way across campus.

The women in Tyler were generally an even mixture of public and private school graduates. One who was very different, however, was the daughter of Madame Homer, diva of the Met at that time. She had her own furniture sent to her room, plus several hundred books. She worked (on writings in Greek) behind her closed and locked door. Actually, she was very shy and was always rather surprised when someone wanted to speak to her. She was interesting.

Another, very different, had won the accolade of "the girl who goes all the way." And, though she was very quiet and mousy, she had plenty of male callers. The fact that she stood out, then, dates her. Today, when male and female students share quarters regularly, she would merely have competition.

The rest of us, then, had rather dissimilar extracurricular activities. I, for example, rode out on my bicycle to visit several elderly shut-ins regularly, and I helped give psychology tests to special students in the public school. And I was a class officer, a job that introduced me to other students.

William Allan Neilson was president of the college at that time. Not a tall man, he was erect, white-haired, with a trim white goatee, and the merry blue eyes of a Scot. He exhorted us, at the weekly general meeting of the college population in John M. Greene Hall, to become scholars like himself, and, of course, to act accordingly. We met with him in smaller groups at the President's House and could appreciate his sense of humor (very erudite) and scholarship in literature and history first-hand.

As one of the youngest in the Class of 1939, I was rather immature socially. I was still only observing my environs and the people in it, and had not disciplined myself toward a definite goal in life, even a definite field. I was merely a passenger on the world, enjoying its fruits—horses, mountains, rivers, books, and drawing, and writing about it all. Would I always be merely an observer of life?

I loved the world I saw through the microscope in zoology lab, the small living organisms with fantastic shapes and life histories, and I liked, too, drawing each specimen just as it was. My professor liked them, too, and kept them for her own use! I was able to keep at the top of the class in the sciences. I kept thinking in terms of being part of a great expedition of discovery in some foreign land—something with some adventure or daring to it. More practically, I could have pursued a medical illustration career, but instead, I floundered along, still wondering what road to take. Courses later in psychology suggested a career in rehabilitation medicine.

Yet, days in the laboratory when I was alone doing assigned experiments on my own time, I often stood at the window looking out at the day, the grass and flowers and the college paths. Would I really want to, or be able to, spend four or more years inside dreary laboratories in old, however hallowed, buildings? On other days, I dreamed of hunting down the cause of cancer, or releasing minds from the prison of schizophrenia. I joined a class of seniors one day on a visit to the neighboring bleak state mental hospital where we were to view the catatonic patients shocked by a recent devastating flood. They stood mute and could be placed in positions, with arms out, for instance, and would simply remain rigidly there. Could I be as detached, though kind, as the physicians there?

That real boyfriend, at last, was also a pre-med student (he had been a blind date.). Completely dedicated to medicine—his father was a doctor—he was a senior at Princeton. At the end of his senior year, he was ready for marriage. I was not. He married a hometown girl who had always wanted him and became a well-known pediatrician.

I graduated still in a quandary. My parents thought a trip to Europe might crystallize a decision, and I would then meet my mother with her family in England. A friend in New Jersey planned to go along on the Italian freighter that would touch the Azores, Spain, Algiers, Sicily and Italy, but she thought Europe looked too warlike and decided not to go.

I went alone.

CHAPTER 3

War

On September 1, 1939, the conjecture, the worry, the gnawing uncertainty were over. Hitler's Nazi armies crossed the border into Poland. Britain declared war two days later.

My mother and I were in England that fateful day, on a more or less regular visit to my mother's family at the end of my freighter trip to Europe during the summer. It turned into a somber visit. Gathered at the historic brick house in the Salisbury Cathedral Close were two uncles, Gen. Fruin Freeth, owner of the house, and Sir Vernon Kell, then head of MI-5, the British Secret Service unit, and a cousin, Geoffrey Allen from the Foreign Office, and their wives. Each night, for the week we were there, the men sequestered themselves with the telephone in the library. The women walked the garden, played a desultory game of croquet, or listened to Mrs. Freeth play the cello. The British, better than we, knew what war would mean.

At each port we visited on my trip in the freighter *Saturnia*, I felt the deep hatred Hitler had already engendered and the simmering intrigue in Europe, especially in the Mediterranean. I befriended a Swiss, Hans Suter, and a Yugoslav, Freddi Baum, who had somehow divided alert passengers into two factions: theirs, against Nazism, and the Germans. I didn't realize this until I sat awhile listening to the Germans aboard playing some music. Hans and Freddi pulled me away.

"You must not support them in any way. They are Nazis."

Then I began to notice the rift between these Germans who were Nazis and the other passengers. The Nazis spoke confidently in loud voices, played loud music, drank, and sang loud songs, while the Europeans glanced at them with hatred and half-closed eyes. I noticed at our stop in Vigo, Spain, that other Germans had turned up on shore—possibly Germans left from the recent devastating Spanish Civil War. In Algiers, as a group of us walked through the Casbah where the uneven walkway was bordered by running sewage and where, in the brothel section, each girl stood forlornly before her red-painted closet of a house, the Germans accosted them while the others quietly passed by. When the ship stopped at Venice, and I sat drinking coffee in St. Mark's Square, I saw what amounted to a marching column, circling the square, singing and clapping loudly.

"Nazis," I heard in disgust around me.

Later I came to recognize, and fear, that marching song in other European towns.

Even with their duties and concerns for their country, the uncles made time to obtain passage for us out of England and back to the United States. It was not easy. Twice our reservations were canceled and changed.

We did not want to run away. I wanted very much to stay and take part. We were discouraged from doing that, however.

"You've read the papers," they said. "Pundits are saying England has virtually four good rifles and three good planes at this moment to defend herself should the Nazis finally turn their war machine upon us—and we do not doubt that they will try. We must be prepared. If you want to help, then work to persuade your country to help us supply ourselves with what we'll need. Though your president sees our need, his Congress and your people are not behind him. You must help there. If you stay here, we will simply have two more mouths to feed." We bid them goodbye, thinking fearfully what lay ahead for them. (All three of them were to lose their lives during the war, Geoffrey Allen at Dunkirk.)

Our refugee ship was the Dutch steamer *Nieuw Amsterdam*. She sailed, loaded down, the night of September 2 from Southampton.

We were assigned to the children's playroom, a large room on the main deck, where fifty mattresses had been laid out on the floor. For women and children only, they were six inches apart. One's baggage sat on the mattress, too. Of toilet facilities, there were three, soon to stop up and leak on the floor. Only dim lights lit the room.

Shortly after pulling away from the pier, amid other ships also overloaded with refugees, those of us who were able-bodied were called upon to help paint the portholes black, to help us pass unseen through the open Channel and beyond.

In the morning, we heard whispered about that another refugee ship, the *Athenia*, had been sunk by a torpedo in the Irish Sea and that many were lost.

I remember little of our voyage except the complaints of nearby ladies who couldn't change their clothes, of crying and uncomfortable babies and children, and that the ship ran out of drinking water and food before we finally passed the Statue of Liberty and entered New York Harbor.

Back in the United States, friends and news commentators were advising that this was Europe's war, that they should not depend on us this time, and the United States should look to her own shores and interests. Even Charles Lindbergh said these things.

Meanwhile, well before Pearl Harbor, those with relatives in Europe sent off food parcels and woolen things ("Bundles for Britain," though not just Britain) and gave blood to the Red Cross. President Roosevelt, convinced that our ultimate entry into the war was inevitable, responded early on to Prime Minister Churchill's needs by devising the Lend-Lease program, which Congress would have to pass, to get ships to Britain.

For me, this was a time to settle down, at last, still with the goal of helping in the war effort ahead. My college preparation had been for a career in medicine. This was the serious and scientific side of a dabbler in adventure. The struggle between these two sides was to became a lifelong contest.

The uncertainty of the times seemed to preclude entering medical school, but I could search for jobs in science. In 1940, the advertised jobs for women were largely for file clerks and typists. I did find one that called for an artist to do animation for medical movies at an old movie studio on Long Island where stripper Gypsy Rose Lee, Robert Benchley, Sylvia Sidney, and others were acting in commercial advertising films. The medical movies in my job turned out to be for instruction in the use of contraceptives of one kind and another. Frame after frame of the movie showed the insertion of these devices into living models. The artist's animation was for drawings showing how they worked. This, plus Gypsy Rose Lee's stories, gave my education quite a boost. There were other movies on nutrition and food. My work was to draw the various breeds of cows—Jersey, Hereford, Fresian—whose milk was being compared.

I lost this job, actually, because of remarks I was heard to make about my German boss. But he did wear his hair like Hitler's, and he had one disconcerting piebald eye.

At home, my mother had been encouraging me to do volunteer work, and so signed me up to drive five disabled children, all about six years old, to the county hospital for weekly treatments. Four had had polio and had been left with paralyzed arms or legs. They sat on the back seat talking in low voices to one another. The fifth, a boy, had muscular dystrophy. He was shy and unsteady. Without seat belts then, I had to drive very carefully, and sometimes had to reach out to keep him from tumbling off the seat.

When we got to the hospital, I helped them all in. Some had to wait until there was a free examination room. I soon learned how the treatments were done and, in fact, usually did them myself while the nurses and doctors "kidded around" with one another. They all received the same treatments. First, as they lay on the examination table, they had to stretch their arms and legs way up, and I would try to help them, trying not to hurt them. Then, they were treated with a plastic vibrator shaped like a claw. It made a crackling noise, and had to be drawn along their little fragile legs and arms to stimulate them. Then everyone got dressed, and we drove home.

Soon I found a medical research job where I would be investigating vitamins. The company extracted vitamins A and B from fish oils and studied, in their laboratory, the effects on rats of various doses, as well as the total absence of all the forms of these vitamins. Papers showing the results of these studies were published in scientific journals. Auxiliary research was done in the company library, based on national and foreign scientific literature and patents. The patents were especially important, as the company was selling its vitamin products.

The company building, a factory actually, was outside of Newark, New Jersey. It was in an area of other factories, and was immediately adjacent to a leather tanning factory which not only stank but leaked a horrid green liquid (the bating solution) down the road where we had to walk. To get a breath of fresh air and a wider view, as it were, I sometimes climbed to the roof of our building. From there, I could see Manhattan and the Hudson River.

One afternoon, which must have been an especially frustrating day, I climbed to the roof to look around. It was a grey day. The tall New York buildings seemed to blend into the cloudy sky. But just above them, in a break in the clouds, where the sky looked silver, was a silhouetted airplane. I watched as it lazily crossed the sky.

"Imagine doing nothing but piloting that airplane across the country, sitting up there and looking at the world stretching away around you," I thought. "I shall learn to fly. Why have I not thought of it before?"

This might be the opening I had been looking for. If I became a commercial pilot, perhaps I could get a job flying an air ambulance. I had read about the Royal Air Force Air Transport Auxiliary women pilots in England. I just might be able to join them if I could fly an air ambulance. This would fulfill both my interest in medicine and my search for adventure. With my job I could pay for flying lessons, and while learning to fly on weekends I could stay to do some work for them, perhaps.

But I didn't know whether my parents, particularly my father, would be enthusiastic about this plan.

This brave new goal called for a divorce from laboratories and libraries. On my own, I moved into an apartment in New York City's Greenwich Village.

Through friends already there, I became acquainted with the young and struggling liberal group of artists and writers. We met at one another's apartments, at small rowdy restaurants, or just in the park at Washington Square. Often our deep discussions into *life* and about the war continued through the night, with, now and then, a few napping on the floor. At this time, early in the war, Communist organizations summoned us to meetings where budding writers were warned that if they did not join up they would never get any editorial job. The Communists would see to that. Some were convinced and joined. I did not. I had no sympathy for the Communists and did not attend another meeting. Nor did I want to be "controlled" by these organized pushy types. I never suffered any dire consequences thereby, anyhow.

I lived, as well, not far from my grandmother and Aunt Fan. Visits with them provided a more conservative balance and opportunities to attend New York plays and concerts with them. They lived on 12th Street, off Fifth Avenue, very close to Eleanor Roosevelt's Greenwich Village apartment. My grandmother was a friend and admirer of hers, and was sympathetic as well to FDR's efforts to equip Britain with destroyers and munitions as they suffered the nightly aerial assault of the Battle of Britain in 1940.

I had changed my job to writing public relations releases for Eastern Air Lines. I also assisted an editor in preparing the monthly edition of the Eastern Air Lines magazine that is tucked into the seat pocket of every Eastern Air Lines plane. Eddie Rickenbacker was still president but, I was told, he disliked women pilots, so I never told him my plans—not that I ever saw much of him. But dashing pilots from the airline and from the military came through. I felt I had entered the world of flying at least.

On a weekend when my parents were away, I drove to the small airport in Basking Ridge, New Jersey. I could at least *ask* about lessons. There were only a few cars parked outside the office building, and all the airplanes seemed to be tied down in a line for the night. But I heard voices, so I entered the office. Two men sat there.

"I'd like to see about flying lessons," I said.

"Well, you are just too late for the Civilian Pilot Training program of the government. They have just eliminated girls from the program," the older man, apparently the owner, said.

"But if you want to fly, we can teach you to fly," the younger man said quickly. "Why not take a trial flight right now? If you like it, we'll count it as your first lesson." And he started out toward the airplanes. This was Lew Penn, who would later be my instructor; subsequently he flew as a captain for Pan American Airlines and crashed mysteriously in the mountains of Brazil.

We untied a yellow Piper Cub airplane. I climbed in the back tandem seat, as directed.

"You will have to help me get the plane started," he said. "While I swing the propeller out front, you will have to stamp hard on the brakes and pull the stick back in your lap, so I don't get run over. The brakes are those little knobs under the rudder pedals."

When the engine started and the plane came to life, Lew jumped in the front seat. We bumped over the rough ground, wings dipping from side to side, as we taxied out for takeoff. I had only flown once, in a Douglas DC-3 airliner (free, as an Eastern Air Lines employee), so this small aircraft, so close to the grass and so fragile-looking, was a new experience. At the end of the runway, Lew ran up the engine, looked carefully for aircraft that might be landing, and then lined up for takeoff.

"Notice what I'm doing on takeoff. Then, when we get up there, you can try it."

As we went faster and faster down the runway, I could hardly tell when we were airborne, except that what had been a waddling duck on the ground was now a sure, smooth craft nosing into the sky. In the quiet evening air, it circled above the office, the trees, the streets and the cars, the smoke from the chimneys, the blue shadows across the grass. The ground was behind us and we were flying in the sparkling air where there was still sunlight. The feeling of freedom when an aircraft takes off may well start a pilot's addiction to flying.

But darkness was filling in around us, and we had to turn back. I touched the controls once or twice, hoping I would show some innate ability to fly. But when Lew brought the plane down on tiptoe, I couldn't feel the moment of touching down. Could I ever do that?

When I got home, the light of the sky continued to fill my mind. I could still feel us drifting above the treetops. I could not sit still. I circled round and round the room, imagining dangerous wartime rescues, flying on and on above the land and the clouds. I felt suddenly more alive.

"This is what I was made for," I told myself.

But there was no time to lose. It was late 1940. Hitler had begun the devastating air attacks that became the Battle of Britain. Already aircraft and pilots, as well as civilians, were being lost in the thousands. Newspapers pictured the dogfights in the night sky over England, and the incredible exploits of the Spitfire and Hurricane fighters against the greater numbers of German aircraft. It was reported that when the British aircraft landed, they were immediately refueled, quickly repaired if needed, and sent right out again to fly and fight. Each night's papers pictured the chaos at the English airports during these night operations. In the intermittent light of searchlights, disabled planes limped in for landing, while refueled planes took off on the same runways, or from the grass in between. Other planes, like patients in the emer-

gency room, were, in the light of held lanterns, being ministered to for perhaps one more flight to shoot down one more "Hun."

The newspapers also showed maps of the steady Nazi advances through
France and Belgium, showed the ships and barges building up along the
French coast and the advance toward now-famous Dunkirk, where the British
Expeditionary forces were trapped with their backs to the sea.

The Admiralty ordered Allied troop carriers to attempt a rescue and called
for volunteers to help. On May 29, 1940, 242 private boats—ranging in size
from 25 to 88 feet, sail and motor—sailed in dense fog from Ramsgate and
dozens of small ports on England's southeastern coast for Dunkirk. Admiral
Ramsey's "Cockleshell Navy" they were called. These volunteer boats, under
cruel air attack, went in close to shore, picked up soldiers until well overloaded, delivered them to the troop transports lying offshore, and returned to
the confusion and terror of battle again and again, without rest. Finally, on June
3, they could do no more, and took up their course for England. Many boats
had been sunk and their owners lost, my cousin Geoffrey Allen among them.

It was after this evacuation of 340,000 men, this "Miracle of Dunkirk," that
Prime Minister Churchill promised that "we shall not flag or fail, we shall go
to the end . . . we shall fight on the beaches, we shall fight on the landing
grounds, we shall fight in the fields and on the streets, we shall fight in the
hills; we shall never surrender."

In the wake of Dunkirk and Churchill's stirring words, Americans began to
recognize Britain's need for the material support President Roosevelt had
been working for. Yet throughout the country people of all ages and persua-
sions were deliberating whether it was better to assist Britain or enter the
war. The America First Society solidly opposed both, but many favored aid to
Britain.

It was not until a Roosevelt "Fireside Chat" on December 16, 1940, when he
disclosed how his idea of Lend-Lease would work that the real change began.
Congress had begun to show interest in aid to Britain when Navy Secretary
Frank Knox suggested providing destroyers and tanks to the already finan-
cially strapped England by trading war material for bases in the British Em-
pire. Then Roosevelt devised a better plan, where Britain would repay "in
kind" after the war—ships for ships, planes for planes. Roosevelt pointed out
that we must support the Allies as the Axis now included Italy and Japan.

"There can be no appeasement with ruthlessness," he said. We must become
"the arsenal of democracy."

The Axis responded that very night to this speech in support of Britain
with their most devastating air attack of the war so far, demolishing much of
historic London, including Old Bailey and eight Christopher Wren churches.
There was special anguish for Prime Minister Churchill and the select few

who knew that British Intelligence had captured and decoded the German cipher machine, the ENIGMA, and therefore had foreknowledge of German plans to attack. To protect this momentous secret (which also provided U-boat discourse), no warning of any kind could be given. Thus it was that Coventry was destroyed in November 1940 while Churchill and the cryptologists at their secret location at Bletchley Park suffered the agony of knowing too much.

Incidentally, 40 miles from Coventry was Brownsover Hall, center of jet research, where the blueprints for Frank Whittle's successful jet engine were housed before being sent to General Electric Company for development in the United States.

CHAPTER 4

Adventure

I climbed the small plane slowly to 3,000 feet in the warm summer air. Farm-land stretched below me, to a fuzzy horizon. Although I had to look carefully to pick it out from other fields and small buildings, I could still see the small Basking Ridge airport.

My assignment was to practice spins. In these early days, students had to learn what caused airplanes to spin and how to recover (most planes, though not military ones, are spin-proof now).

After turning to check for other airplanes below, behind, or beside, I slowed the engine and pulled the nose high to stall the flight of the plane. (The plane can be stalled at high speed as well.) When it began to buffet, I pulled sharply back on the stick and pushed hard on the right rudder. The plane fell off to the right, nose straight down, so the ground was directly below the propeller and spinning. I moved the stick forward, pushed on the opposite—left—rudder, and gave it throttle to recover from the spin.

As it slowed the spin, however, I suddenly saw that, below me, instead of a revolving propeller, was a stationary wooden prop.

"They sometimes do that," Lew, my instructor had said cheerfully when he demonstrated the spin. "You just need to dive and give it power to get it started again."

This I did repeatedly, but it did not start. We were gliding quietly, my plane and I, and losing altitude. I looked around for the airport and started to plan.

But what had brought me to this sort of situation? I mused, as I floated powerlessly and noiselessly above the New Jersey farmland.

I thought of all the things I had been interested in as I grew up. And they all seemed to have the aura of adventure. Now there was the added impetus to become part of the war effort, in some way.

First there had been the lesson in courage and responsibility at the Colorado ranch with my cowpony Comrade. Then I had done some serious mountain climbing, joined canoeing expeditions in Maine, ridden and trained thoroughbred horses, and traveled around prewar Europe alone. I looked at some of the jobs I had taken after college. I had joined a professional dance group for a while. The fun of that was the sort of places where we performed —cold and drafty schools, little churches, and Lions' Clubs. My first editorial job was as a reader for a literary agent of sorts, Thomas Uzzell. There I chose one manuscript that I thought should be sold. It became the best-selling children's book *My Friend Flicka*. Soon after that Uzzell decided to retire.

Afterward, I wrote features for the *New York Times,* and later had the first page of the *New York Times Magazine* to myself, calling it "About New York." It presented commentary, profiles, and a poem or two. To find material, I explored "about New York" and asked a lot of questions. It was exciting to say, "I'm from the *Times* . . ." but I didn't know when I was well off. I wanted (and needed) a steady job and steady pay.

My last job before leaving for the WASPs was closer to the war effort than I first realized. As a writer for Rockefeller Center Inc., one of my duties was to note the arrival of new corporate tenants and tell their stories.

One day my boss, Merle Crowell, said, "Don't attempt to cover the 36th floor. It's been taken over for secret government work." Only later I learned that this floor housed William Stephenson's British Security Coordination, a spy operation in cooperation with Gen. Bill Donovan's Office of Strategic Services. It was the most secret, most successful intelligence enterprise of World War II, and its exploits are told in William Stevenson's *A Man Called Intrepid.* William Stephenson, while building planes in the 1930s, had helped Frank Whittle with the jet engine later used in the XP-59A jet.

When it came time to leave for duty with the WASPs, Merle Crowell warned that I was jeopardizing a career as a writer if I left then. I would lose all my contacts and my writing skills! But I had already signed up to go, and I was eager to be off to try to do my part in the war.

These were the sorts of "adventure" things that could have finally led to flying, I thought.

The mountains were important, if only for their broad view from the heights. First I had as inspiration an English aunt who allegedly was the first woman to climb the 14,000-foot Matterhorn. After the foothills of the Colorado Rockies, where one had to climb slowly in the high altitudes, I next met the mountains of the Presidential Range in the Northeast. Here I strove to be first of the group to reach the top, first to see the peaks stretching away one beyond the other, with deep blue shadows in between. I had learned the names and shapes of all the key Himalayan peaks and had followed each Everest expedition beginning with Mallory and Irvine. They were the ones who had originally said they climbed Everest "because it was there."

And I remembered once, in Switzerland in 1939, I had a somewhat mystical experience. I had railwayed to the top and, ashamed, decided to walk down. I was the last person allowed on the mountain as dusk fell. I followed cairns across the rocky snow-patched summit; then, below the timberline, I entered dark forests of tall pines, negotiated deep gullies, rushing streams, and slippery turns. As I had been reading *Jean Christophe* by Romain Rolland (a student favorite), I tried composing music as I descended, and I half expected to see some magical person appear around the next turn. But I saw no one. (And in today's violent world, it would have possibly been dangerous if I had.) I reached the railroad station at the bottom in time for the last train to Lucerne, well after dark. (My muscles were stiff for days.)

Addressing myself now to the problem at hand, with a careful turn I pointed the dead airplane toward the airport. I had roughly five miles to go in distance, with about 2,500 feet in altitude remaining. As it was a warm, mushy day, and I might not reach the airport, I picked out a field flat enough and big enough to land in. I had practiced this with my instructor too. But not with a still propeller and a dead engine.

I had to guard against flattening my glide and stalling the airplane, for pulling the nose too high drains away flying speed and the plane stalls. Actually, I enjoyed this challenge! I could hardly wait to see whether I would be able to handle it.

In much the same way, I had approached the challenge of a day of fox hunting. Although it might seem remote from flying, there were indeed connections between the requirements and challenges of fox hunting and flying. (One "flies" over the fences, for example.) Trashed as a nasty "blood sport" by "animal lovers," both here and in England, where I have hunted, nevertheless, it is a stirring sport of ancient tradition and primitive instincts. I enjoyed it as a young girl of 17, and I look back on it nostalgically now.

While it was still dark, I would mount my shining, well-turned-out horse, and ride him, as he spooked at every noise, to the Meet of the Hunt. (Anyone in the neighborhood with a horse was welcome.) Other horses would be milling about. The Huntsman arrived with his babbling, impatient hounds. We moved about, too, settling down our horses, greeting the Master of Hounds and each other.

Once the hounds picked up the scent of the fox and the Huntsman had blown on his horn the quick notes of the "Gone Away," it would be me and my horse at a gallop, up and down hill, over fences—some tricky, some done well, some not so well. Then we would both tire, sometimes following horses, sometimes in the forefront. As my mount became muddy and began to sweat, the horse smell was strong, the reins slippery, but I was firm and down in the saddle. When the scent was lost, and at last we could rest, my horse was watching. He could see the hounds find again before I could, and he recognized the "Gone Away."

Before the day was finished—and the fox had once again eluded the hounds —my horse and I had kept up, chosen a proper line across country, seen the hills brighten in the sun, the dew-covered foliage glisten, heard the crows warn the fox that the hunt is coming, even perhaps given a timid horse a lead over a fence. What remained was a quiet walk home with loose reins and lengthened stirrups.

This sport quickens response, tests riding and judgments skills, exercises the mind and emotions, and touches the edge of danger.

Those who object to this so-called blood sport do not see that, on the unusual occasion of the fox's being caught, the wily varmint has, in a few hours' time, demonstrated his endurance, his magnificent strategies, and his admirable defiance, as have the hounds. Some foxes become legends. Better this than suffering alone in a painful trap.

No, I decided, it was not simply by chance that in the end I chose aviation. My attorney-engineer father had been involved in the patent for the joy-stick—the combined aileron and elevator control in an airplane—and had become an enthusiast of early aviation. On his travels, he flew the developing airlines, often sitting in the copilot seat, in good weather and bad. As a special excursion, he took my small brother and me to watch the mail planes of the early thirties come into Newark Airport at night. We watched the dark plane appear out of the night, its throaty engine backfiring at the slow speed, saw it roll to a stop before the office shack and the pilot jump down. After the plane was fueled, the pilot took it away again, off into the night sky.

Even before the Colorado reunion, our father had driven us out to Hadley Airport in New Jersey, to watch Clarence Chamberlin, who hoped to fly to Paris for the Raymond Orteig prize before Lindbergh, testing the plane he would fly. That day, one wheel dropped off on takeoff, but he did land safely.

When Lindbergh returned from his successful flight in 1927 my father took us into New York to watch Lindbergh's ticker-tape parade from a window in his office, high above Broadway.

In addition, shortly after her Atlantic flight in 1932, Amelia Earhart came to speak at our school. She stood on the stage in a dark maroon dress with a white collar, and told us about meeting bad weather part way across, and how she had to decide whether or not to continue. Was her altimeter correct? Could she escape the waves if she descended below the rain clouds?

As I sat in the front row, enthralled, she came forward and looked right down at me.

When she was lost near Howland Island in the Pacific on her last flight in 1937, we listened to the radio reports for the many days the search for her continued. (We still read all the theories—rational and irrational—about her demise.)

Aiding and abetting this trend toward adventure were some of the books I read: Joseph Conrad's faraway sea voyages, Walter Scott's desert skirmishes, John Buchan's tales of the Scottish hills, Jules Verne's escapes from the earth, and Antoine de Saint Exupery on the "witchery" of flying.

This was all behind me, already ingrained in me before I ever learned to fly.

And now, as I approached the diminutive grass airport, I could see other small yellow aircraft taking off and landing. I had no radio in the plane with which to warn them that I was "dead stick." I would simply have to fit myself in. But I could see I would be too high. I started an easy spiral down, then quickly leveled off as I was losing altitude too fast.

I had to enter the traffic pattern and I could make no mistakes. I turned in where I could make a straight-in approach, to give myself time to line up with the runway. But heat was rising from the flat field and I was not coming down fast enough. I would overreach the runway. There was, however, a crossing runway. It was longer, but not directly into the wind.

I slipped the plane sharply to the right (a maneuver where you cross controls), and the plane touched down silently, giving me room to turn safely at the end of the runway.

Little did I suspect that only two years later, in 1943, I would have an engine quit in an Air Force dive-bomber on takeoff—and have to get *it* back on the runway. Perhaps this rehearsal helped in that later test, to give me confidence to calmly solve the problem. That, or the will to survive kicks in.

CHAPTER 5
Women Airforce Service Pilots (WASPs)

In 1941, like a virulent disease, the war spread throughout Europe. Hitler's armies moved into Denmark and Norway, Yugoslavia and North Africa. U-boat attacks and bombings of England continued, but perhaps because the United States Congress on March 11 finally passed the Lend-Lease Bill, and destroyers and planes began to give support to Britain, Hitler decided to invade Russia. It was said that he believed the war in Russia would only take three months, and then he could concentrate on absorbing England.

Several other theories exist on why Hitler postponed a final attack on England. One, according to William Stephenson (*A Man Called Intrepid*) is that an astrologer trained by British Intelligence was able to convince Hitler it was not the time to defeat England. Another, according to writer John Toland and others, is that Hitler believed the German and the English were of similar stock and should unite rather than fight, and that Rudolf Hess, flying solo to Scotland, was actually Hitler's emissary for peace. (Long before he wrote his biography of Hitler, I met Toland on the train I was taking to Houston to join the WASPs. He argued that a writer should keep himself free to write the story of the war, not fight in it.)

At any rate, Russia was important to Hitler as it would provide the *Lebensraum* he sought for Germany. And on June 22, the world saw Hitler's armies —ignoring the treaty with Stalin—start an advance that in only a month reached Smolensk, just 200 miles from Moscow.

We could feel the concern and dread growing in the United States. After the infamous bombing of Pearl Harbor by Japan on December 7, the country was at last united behind the war effort. The United States and Great Britain declared war on Japan immediately, and we declared war on Germany and Italy as well, while we patrolled the West Coast against attack by Japan.

Roosevelt and Churchill were in constant communication and had, we learned later, secretly met off Newfoundland, where they signed the Atlantic Charter declaring the principles for world peace after defeat of the Nazis. Later, twenty-six Allied nations signed as the "United Nations," avowing not to make separate treaties.

Conscription into the armed forces began in earnest, as did rationing of sugar and rubber and the freezing of the price of steel. Production of planes and tanks in converted auto factories revved up and union leader Walter Reuther pledged no strikes. As the men went off to war, we of the citizenry learned to manage with our ration books for gasoline and food, and bought U.S. Savings Bonds.

War books like William Shirer's *Berlin Diary*, Joseph Davies's *Mission to Moscow*, and Winston Churchill's *Blood, Sweat and Tears* appeared, and songs like "White Christmas," "White Cliffs of Dover," "Paper Doll," and "I'll Be Seeing You" were sung.

Though 1942 began with depressing news from all fronts—heavy losses at Guadalcanal and Bataan and setbacks on the Russian front, certain other daring battles lifted the spirits of the Allies and those at home. Maj. Gen. Jimmy Doolittle led his carrier-based B-25 bomber squadron all the way to Tokyo. The U.S. fleet defeated Japan at Midway. The Allies began night bombardment of German cities. And on November 8, the Allies landed an expeditionary force in North Africa to engage and defeat Rommel's German armies there. At last, as historian Doris Kearns Goodwin said, "We are striking back!"

Meanwhile, in Germany, Allied Intelligence made two disturbing discoveries—that millions of Jews had been exterminated in Nazi gas chambers and that Germany was developing the capability to launch the V-1 and V-2 pilotless rockets in a final effort to subdue England.

In the United States "Rosie the Riveter" had become the national heroine. Women were replacing men in every facet of industry and performing excellently. Eleanor Roosevelt saw that this work could be a success only if there were planned daycare facilities for children. Henry Kaiser was first to provide this at his Swan Island Center in Oregon. Women were also enlisting in the WAVES (Women Accepted for Voluntary Emergency Service in the Navy) and WAAC (Women's Army Auxiliary Corps).

My mother and other housewives contributed by working at the Red Cross as contacts between soldiers and their families or simply as clerks (they all wore blue uniforms), or they grew and froze vegetables and meat, or saved grease or aluminum or rubber. My father was appointed by Civil Defense as an airplane spotter. Every night he served on the midnight to four watch, "spotting" and reporting any aircraft in the vicinity, and I went with him.

Our spotting post was in a tower of a large country house. After parking the car behind the big stone building, we entered a designated door. After passing through silent halls with closed doors, we climbed four stories to the dark tower. We relieved the former watch, signed in, and settled down to watch and listen. Our only light was a flashlight, when necessary. We had a telephone, a pad and pencil, and a pair of binoculars. Every once in a while, we heard the drone of a plane and reported its direction, probable altitude and speed, and guessed its type. It could be an enemy plane.

Otherwise, we spent the long cold hours looking out at the stars. My amateur-astronomer father introduced me to various constellations, to special stars like Sirius, brightest in the heavens, and to the North star, which over the ages has been different stars. Being a friend of Dr. Edwin Hubble, he knew the latest theories of the early universe and what its end might be. All this made celestial navigation, learned much later for the ocean-sailing my husband and I were to do, much more meaningful, and it was an introduction to the mysteries of space.

My particular project, now that I had my private pilot's license, was to build up the 200 hours of flying time required for a commercial license—the ticket to a job in aviation. I still had my eye on an assignment to an air ambulance. I bought half an airplane with another aspiring private pilot, Jasper Wright, and we alternated in the use of our tired old Piper Cub (underpowered, no brakes, tears in the fabric) and flew, flew, flew.

It was certainly not an unpleasant task to have to go out and fly with a purpose in view, and even in one's own plane, though the plane was somewhat of a wreck. That added to the challenge. The last figures in its official number on the wing ended in "48," and it was known around the airport as "good old 48." Its engine popped and banged on the glide to land just like a P-51 fighter.

Some days I would simply go up and sightsee, enjoy the farmland below, and reach up to the scattered clouds above. Other times, I practiced flying maneuvers like lazy eights, wingovers, spins. I visited airports in the area. I flew in good weather and bad.

I did more serious flying for the national Civil Air Patrol. We not only practiced rescue missions and patrols but, as the war progressed, actually performed them. I introduced Boy Scouts and Girl Scouts to the joy of flying. I took my brother and my mother for rides, but my father never flew with me. He thought I would be nervous.

As I closed in on the magic number 200 in the summer of 1942, all private flying on the Eastern seaboard was prohibited because submarines had been seen offshore. Airplanes had to be dismantled, wings off, so they could not be flown at all.

Then I saw a news story explaining how the Air Force planned to use experienced women pilots for domestic military flying in order to release men for active duty overseas. Eleanor Roosevelt, in her "My Day" newspaper column on September 1, 1942, said that "women pilots are a weapon waiting to be used."

Back in July 1941, Jacqueline Cochran, already famous for her speed records and Harmon trophies, and, in fact, the leading woman pilot of the nation, had presented to Secretary of War for Air Robert Lovett (at the suggestion of President Roosevelt) a plan for using woman pilots to ferry new trainer-type aircraft to air bases, thus freeing men for more active roles. Lovett passed it on to Gen. H. H. "Hap" Arnold, Chief of the Air Force.

"How many experienced women pilots are there?" General Arnold asked.

Cochran and her staff laboriously checked through Civil Aeronautical Administration files and found that of 2,733 licensed women, 150 had over 200 hours flying time—and between 72 and 100 had 300 hours and over. She sent questionnaires to these pilots asking whether they would be interested in serving with the Air Corps (the Air Corps became the Air Force after Pearl Harbor). "Yes," 130 answered enthusiastically. On July 30, Cochran presented a finished proposal to Col. Robert Olds, head of the Ferry Command of the Air Transport Command, for an "Organization of a Women Pilots' Division of the Army Air Corps Ferry Command." After all, she pointed out, women were successfully ferrying aircraft for the Royal Air Force in Britain, and in Russia women pilots were even flying combat missions (albeit with high losses) in tiny, old biplanes.

"An experimental group of experienced women pilots in the United States might begin immediately flying small trainers from factories to bases," she wrote.

General Arnold told Jackie (as she was known) that the Air Corps was not ready for or needful of women pilots, but suggested that she fulfill the request of the British Air Transport Auxiliary that she recruit American women pilots for them. She was able to deliver twenty-five women pilots with 300 hours or more flying time, all of whom would sign a contract for 18 months' duty in England. By August 1942 they were processed in Canada and went to England by ship.

While Cochran was in England another well-known woman aviator (who had been flying since 1936), Nancy Harkness Love, took a different tack. She recruited forty-nine women commercial pilots with at least 500 hours in many different airplanes (they were called ships then) who would gladly serve in the Ferry Command, and right away, and presented it to Colonel Olds.

This plan, too, ran into difficulties, not the least of which was a change in Air Force personnel. Colonel (now General) Olds moved up as head of the Second Air Force. Brig. Gen. Harold George replaced him, and under him, as head of the Ferrying Division of the Air Transport Command, was Col. William Tunner. At the same time the needs of the Air Force changed. In 1942, they found themselves short of ferry pilots, and new planes were accumulating at the factories. Love was asked to submit a new proposal for hiring women ferry pilots, including their qualifications and how they would be used.

"But how would they be paid, and would they be hired on the same basis as civilian men pilots?" Tunner wanted to know.

Unfortunately they could not be an arm of the WAAC, as the WAAC had no provision for flying personnel. The men were hired from civilian flying jobs for a 90-day trial, after which they were commissioned into the Air Force. It was decided that the women would simply be hired as provisional Civil Service employees, but they were promised that the Air Force would "go to bat for them later" in Congress to make them part of the Air Force. While the men were to be paid $380 per month, the women would be paid $250. The men needed only 200 flying hours to be hired, the women 500. The men did not even need a high school diploma.

General George was satisfied with the proposal as worked out with Colonel Tunner. The Women's Auxiliary Ferry Troop (later Squadron, or WAFS) was born, so to speak, with Nancy Love at its head. Final approval would, of course, have to come from General Arnold. But Love confidently sent telegrams on September 10, 1942, to her cadre of experienced women pilots to report to the New Castle (Delaware) Army Air Base. Twenty-eight of her highly qualified young women arrived.

Cochran arrived home from England, furious. She demanded of General Arnold to know what was going on.

General Arnold had changed his mind about women pilots. He had approved Love's plan for the WAFS and, after listening patiently to Cochran's arguments, also backed the training plan she outlined. He saw that the war was expanding and there would be a need for more ferry pilots to augment the WAFS. As she had planned, Cochran would be chief of her training group. It would be called the 319th Women's Flying Training Detachment and would be stationed at the Municipal Airport in Houston, Texas.

At that point there were two women pilot organizations operating in the United States, plus the English contingent. But by July 5, 1943, after Cochran's training program proved itself, and women graduates began to enter other flying duties besides ferrying, all women pilots in the Army Air Forces—those in training and those flying for Air Transport Command— were under the sole jurisdiction of the director of women pilots, Jacqueline Cochran. Nancy Love would direct the women of ATC. The consolidation was called Women's Airforce Service Pilots, or WASPs, and all would wear the blue uniforms designed by Cochran.

Still, Cochran's hope for militarization of her pilots—and the rights that went with it—was not realized, nor would it be until the 1970s, long after the war. Eleanor Roosevelt, worrying that men serving their country in World War II had lost years in which they could prepare for careers and families, had urged the president to pass the G.I. Bill of Rights. The bill provided that the government would underwrite education and training for returning veterans. The WASPs, as Civil Service, would not be eligible.

Nancy Love and Jackie Cochran were very different, and had different conceptions of what an Air Force woman pilot should be and what she should do.

Nancy Love grew up in the affluent Harkness family in Boston and married Robert Love, of similar background and interests. They were cruising and racing sailors in New England waters, while they ran Intercity Airlines in Boston, for which Nancy was a pilot. She had flown with other women pilots for the Bureau of Air Commerce to airmark rooftops with names of towns and arrows pointing in their direction as aids to navigation to cross-country flyers. She had always had a plane of her own to fly, and most of the commercial pilots she had recruited were her personal friends.

As Sally Van Wagenen Keil in *Those Wonderful Women in Their Flying Machines* describes her, Love was content to get her group into the Ferry Command and to keep her WAFS as an elite group. She took good care of them, in the early days supplying them with grey-green uniforms and hats, and continuously seeing to it that they flew better and better aircraft. She even tried to get them—and herself—on transatlantic flights, but General Arnold rejected that request, then and for the duration of the war (despite the general but erroneous belief that WAFS or WASPs "flew bombers to England").

Jackie Cochran, on the other hand, started out life as an orphan (it is alleged that she never knew who her parents were) and lived in foster homes in the lumbermill towns of Florida. Early on she learned to fight for what she wanted. After working as a beautician, she formed and ran her own Jacqueline Cochran Cosmetic Company. When she learned to fly, her forte was breaking speed and altitude records and she entered and won transcontinental and speed races formerly entered only by men. She was encouraged all along the way by her husband, businessman Floyd Odlum.

"Elite" was not a word that interested Cochran. Her group would be businesslike, well organized, fair, and proficient. Their training would be, in fact, the same training Air Force cadets got—same airplanes, same hours, same ground school. And all women would have the same training, before graduation, regardless of former experience. They would, in fact, be professionals, the first such women flyers. So not only did they benefit the war effort, but they received training for a new profession. Every WASP would, in fact, have gladly served as a WASP without pay.

In spite of their differences, Cochran and Love respected one another and worked together for the duration.

Although I had never met Nancy Love in the war years, much later, in 1947 or so, I rowed over from our sailboat to hers in a quiet harbor in Maine, and asked her how she felt about her years in the Ferry Command. Disappointingly, she said she "was simply glad to have a rest now," but that she had admired all her recruits, who, she said, did so much better than Cochran's trainees. I could have reminded her that official reports had shown just the opposite, but I rowed back instead.

And in the summer of 1948, Mary Margaret McBride asked me to join Jackie Cochran on her radio program. I can remember the year well as I was 8.99 months pregnant with our second child, and looked it. Mary Margaret was much more interested in this fact than any aspect of the flying, and in fact hoped for a birth on her show. (Jackie was not particularly interested in that, however.)

Overall, 25,000 young women jumped at the chance to fly planes as a WASP to help in the war effort. Very few of them fulfilled the basic requirements: to be an American citizen, be between 21 and 35 years old, have approximately 200 flying hours (later it would be less), be able to pass a stiff Air Force physical exam, and, most important, satisfy in an interview Cochran's pattern of what a future WASP should be. Only 1,800 were selected, and, of them, 1,070 would graduate.

The accepted applicants came from every conceivable background. Actresses, golf champions, journalists, a blackjack dealer, teachers, secretaries, relatives of men already in service, nurses, biologists, a bartender, all applied.

But what was the common denominator?

According to Deborah Douglas, author of the National Air and Space Museum–Smithsonian Institution report "U.S. Women in Aviation, 1940–1985," "Cochran's interview was used to assess the candidate's personality, her stability, and various aspects of her background that might be an indication of her future performance under stress."

It was a cold winter day, late in 1942, when I reported to Jackie Cochran's Manhattan apartment overlooking the East River. With me was Susan Ford, a sometime riding companion who had many hundreds more flying hours than I. As the elevator opened on Jackie's floor, we saw probably thirty young hopefuls milling around, many examining the Harmon trophies on display. A friendly woman (we later learned her name—Ethel Sheehy) gave us questionnaires to fill out. Then we would be interviewed, first, by Sheehy or Laoti Deaton and then, presumably if approved, by Cochran. Of course our flight logs would be checked, too. Susan wasn't as worried about the outcome as I, as she already knew Jackie and needed no interview. Surprisingly, Jackie's interview was short, friendly, but very businesslike—just a few questions and the admonition that there would be risks we'd have to face. Examining this famous, handsome, blonde flyer and achiever, I asked myself, 'Could I ever resemble her?'

Sue was simply sent home to pack, as she would go to the Air Transport Auxiliary in England. It was shortly before Christmas that I received my orders to report to Houston in January 1943 to be in the Class of 43-W-3.

What a Christmas present!

CHAPTER 6

In Service

The war began to take a more encouraging turn in 1943. In the beginning of that year, the Japanese were driven from Guadalcanal and the German armies were bogged down in Stalingrad. The British Eighth Army was advancing in Africa. And Roosevelt and Churchill had met secretly in Casablanca and decided that their next move would be to attack Sicily—to knock Italy out of the war—rather than to try a cross-Channel attack at this time.

In the United States, the new women pilot training organization had just entered the great war machine against the Nazi and Japanese aggression now spread over much of the globe. In the Air Force Ferry Command, these women moved planes from factories to bases, and in Houston a new contingent of trainees arrived each month for training.

The young women, excited and eager to play a serious part in the war effort, found their new base bleak and unpromising. The picture in their minds of an active Air Force training base, with lines of silver planes, the noise of engines starting up, the nearby barracks, the crowd of fellow pilots, was dashed by the tired hangar that was all that housed Aviation Enterprises Ltd., where their orders led them. Cochran had not yet found anything but this rather rundown pilot training base for her first recruits. Makeshift offices were hidden away in tiny outbuildings. And where was the mess hall? Where were the barracks? The infirmary? In fact, where were the planes?

The Aviation Enterprises Ltd. hangar stood off the end of one runway of the Houston Municipal Airport. There were some benches and tables out front, along the taxiway. Some young women in motley costumes sat there, watching as my class—the third Houston class—straggled in from the train station in the middle of January 1943.

In answer to our first question, they told us, "Yes, this is it, believe it or not.

You report to Deaton over there," and one of them pointed to a small building attached to the hangar. The speaker was Byrd Granger, of the first class (who would later make a compendium of histories of every class called *On Final Approach*).

"Airplanes? There they are in front of you—all those Piper Cubs, Taylorcrafts and Aeroncas. They do promise us Air Force trainers, some day. We keep looking for them.

"The instructors? They hate us to begin with, and they hate flying the Cubs as well. You may not learn much from them.

"Oh, and if you need to use the bathroom, you walk up there to the Municipal Terminal Building. And for meals, we stagger up to that honky-tonk restaurant."

"Where do we live?" The women laughed and looked knowingly at one another.

"You'll see," another one, tall with greying hair, joked. "I'm Margery Gray, and they'll pick you up by bus—actually a covered truck—after supper here and then deposit you at your *grand* living quarters."

"Some of us have cars that we're still allowed to drive, though," a neat and tidy blonde said. "We try to fill them as full as we can. I'm Sidney Miller. We're all from the first class. Oh, here come the second-class girls!"

A line of small planes taxied in from the runway. Everyone watched them circle to face the taxi strip. We watched the propellers stop and the occupants climb out of the planes. As they walked by, lugging their parachutes over their shoulders, we studied them and their instructors. None of them looked thrilled with the flight.

One made a face, leaned toward Sidney, and cupped her hand over her mouth. "I have over 300 hours of flying time, but after that damn guy yells at me all afternoon I always land the plane like a beginner. I even skid in turns. Oh God!"

"These are third-class girls . . ."

"Oh, hi—I'm Mary Trotman. You're going to *love* it here," and she walked after the others.

We "third-class girls," dragging our suitcases, found Dedie Deaton and checked in.

"Well, welcome. Put your bags over by the shed there. They'll be taken with you all when the bus takes you to your living quarters." Rather harried, she looked down at some notes. "You'll be living in nice motels nearer town. I'm just now making out the list. Some of you are already in your houses. Now go with the other girls to the restaurant for supper."

About ten of us had gathered on the road to the restaurant. Having paid our way here, we would now pay for our meals. Our pay, as trainees, would be $150 per month.

It was dark by the time we were delivered to our motels, so we didn't see them clearly. And it took a little time to sort out everyone—there were to be sixty-eight of us—and each motel was filled to capacity with women pilots. We found why the Class 1 women were laughing. We had been assigned to double rooms with but one bed, so we were two in a bed!

Although everyone had had a tiring trip down, regardless of the means of transportation, women thrown together for any reason talk and question and exclaim until voices and laughter reach high decibels. Indeed, there was much to talk about, conjecture about.

My room (and bed) -mate was a short, dark-haired, lively young woman from Texas, Lois Hollingsworth. She had been a flying instructor. In an adjoining room were two friends who had asked to share a room (but not a bed!), Frances Grimes, a laboratory scientist, and Gretchen Gorman, a quiet girl who seldom participated in the conversation. Frances and I shared an interest in "space" and "what's out there," and often traded theories after the others had turned in.

But this night, all the other W-3s in our motel had found places to sit, on the bed, on the floor, on the desk, to join the discussion in our room. The diversity was wonderful. Mary Lee Leatherbee was an actress (and sister of producer Joshua Logan) whose husband had recently died. Emma Coulter, from the horsy part of Pittsburgh, was an animal lover who once transported a black bear—in her car—across the country to Arizona where, now that he was too big to live around the house, he would be in a bear refuge. Margaret Cook, with curly brown hair in the Amelia Earhart style, taught school in Alaska. Kay Menges, tall, brunette, with lots of flying hours, was a fellow New Jersey pilot. Dora Dougherty, bright, humorous, had an engineering background and would later be checked off in the B-29 bomber. Jean Pearson wrote for the *Detroit Free Press* and, much later, was my maid of honor when I married.

"What have we got ourselves into?" was the basic question, but no one in the room was ready to give it up (though a few others had left when confronted with two in a bed). Most all the new trainees had been the "only girl pilot at the airport," and adjusting to the competition of others was as humbling as it had been in college finding that the other students had been tops of their high school classes, too. In fact, adjusting to the rules and regulations of "army" life was going to be hard for young women who were accustomed to the freedom to run their own lives.

Already we had learned something about one another—who would be a leader (we chose Menges), who would be the jolly one, the clown who would turn the bad things into comedies (we chose Leatherbee), and perhaps also who might not pass. It was hard to picture any of us as a military pilot.

There were discouraging days. The two upper classes had prepared us. The planes were old, the instructors indeed hated us. The food was bad. The upper classes avoided us. We didn't seem to be progressing.

And we might have failed if a young lieutenant, Alfred Fleischman, had not stepped in. He was not even part of the Women's Flying Training Detachment then. He was assigned to an army supply depot next door, when he offered to assist Dedie Deaton in training the new recruits. He started by giving us calisthenics each day, then taught us to march in the military manner (at first we thought marching was silly). But mostly he stiffened our backs, lifted us out of our self-pity, and, in fact, inspired us to do a good job.

"This is no boarding school," he said. "There is an army directive, which, if you follow it, will keep you in good physical and mental health: 'If the Army can dish it out, I can take it.' If you can't take it, you will affect this whole experiment to use women to fly military planes to help in the war effort."

Even though we were a special experiment, with no uniform except our own khaki trousers, white shirt, and overseas cap (and our surplus Air Force faded flying coveralls two sizes too big), Fleischman had challenged us. We now had something to prove.

One evening, just before dusk, just before we were to board our bus to return to our motels, a sleek, silver plane touched down and taxied to the flight line. Then another. And another.

"They're PT-19s! Our first Air Force trainer!"

We drove off with a cheer and a song.

New instructors arrived, too. Recruited from around Texas and nearby flying schools, they were excellent. One was a woman, Helen Duffy, and one, Judson Palmer, was probably the best instructor I ever had. Not long afterward, some more advanced planes arrived, too, the Vultee BT-13 basic trainer. It had a canopy over the cockpit and had propeller pitch control that gave it a marvelously noisy sound, a sound with authority.

Now, at last, we felt we were on our way. We were a flying training school. We were flying the same primary trainers, (the Fairchild PT-19) and basic trainers (the Vultee BT-13) as every Air Force cadet in training.

We were also enrolled in similar ground school courses—navigation, engine operation, meteorology, and Morse code. Our navigation teacher, Grace P. Hilliard, was an admiral's daughter and she, too, had Navy connections. She was small and dark, very direct, very strict, and impressed upon us the importance of *perfect* navigation, especially for future ferry pilots.

We learned engine operation by taking apart and rebuilding a real engine.

Meteorology could be studied right outside in Houston's panoply of weather —its fogs, fronts, thunderstorms, inversions, and temperature changes. Only icing conditions were absent.

Morse code was taught by a former ship's radio operator and amateur radio ham. Rather resembling an owl (we could picture him listening to the dot dash throughout the night), he would not tolerate a lack of appreciation of the need to learn code expertly. What we did learn was that it took total concentration to master it. And it was essential because radio range stations and beacons for radio navigation in instrument conditions and at night were identified by Morse code letters. One must identify the calls correctly. Code is also used for emergency messages and on shipboard.

After ground school, we marched back to the flight line, sometimes practicing "to the rear, march" or "double time, march" on the way, but not very smartly.

Flying the streamlined PT-19, we could easily imagine we were flying fighters. It was responsive, it had power, and in a turn you could look straight down the wing to the ground. It was even hard to make a bad landing in it. And it would be the last airplane we would fly with the wind in our faces in an open cockpit. We flew long cross-country flights solo, and in the moments of terror when we weren't sure where we were over Texas we had to clutch the chart as we checked it so it wouldn't blow out of the cockpit.

The BT-13 was heavier, with more power and the added propeller pitch control. Our instructor, Palmer this time, took about ten of us out to a small grass field to try out the plane. We took turns flying, with Palmer, our turns and stalls and landings. I was the only one to solo that first day.

But my "prowess" was short-lived. The next day I had a rash and a sore throat. Our only medic was an itinerant nurse. She said, "Measles." There was nowhere to quarantine me except back at the motel. I stayed in a room by myself for the proper period, my only nourishment being milkshakes brought to the window, kindly, by fellow WASPs. I don't know what temperature I had, but the sore throat got worse. Finally, I called a doctor whose name I found in the telephone book. Rather than coming to see me, he sent out some sulfa pills.

"Take them all," he said. "You'll be fine."

But when the quarantine time was up, and the pills were gone and I was called back to the flight line, I was far from "fine." The world was tilting around me and voices seemed to echo in my head. I could hardly drag myself around.

"Just take any BT and fly around to get used to it again," Palmer said.

"I don't think I'm ready to fly solo," I ventured.

Palmer laughed. I picked up my parachute and walked out to the airplane. Struggling up the wing and into the cockpit, I looked around and tried to remember what to do.

I started it up and taxied out, checked the controls and engine, and turned on to the runway. I was cleared for takeoff.

I "poured the coal to it," as they say, and sped down the runway. I realized suddenly that I was in the air. I noticed also that my air speed was dangerously low. I dropped the nose. Then, as I gained altitude, I noticed one wing was low. My air speed dropped again. I dropped the nose, lifted the wing.

I realized I had no feeling of the altitude or speed of the aircraft whatsoever. I could only mechanically monitor it, and if I didn't do it in time . . .

Going from too slow to too fast, to too low to too high, from level flight to banking, I struggled to keep in the flying pattern. Somehow I would have to land. I could not fly.

Turning on my final approach, I cut back on the engine and let the nose drop. I fought to keep it level, not to stall. Finally, I lined it up with the proper runway and let it land itself. It only bounced a little. I taxied back and cut the engine.

"I don't think I'm ready," I told Palmer.

"I know. I saw you. I was praying for you. Better check with the nurse."

When it was found that I essentially had no red blood cells and few white ones as well, I was sent home to New York, to, it was hoped, be made well. First stop was Memorial Hospital, to check for leukemia. With a tiny drill, marrow was withdrawn from my breastbone and examined. Other fancy tests were done. The decision was "nothing serious." The problem was caused by too much unmonitored sulfa medicine. In two months of eating and drinking liver night and day, and riding a horse and walking, I built myself up again.

But I had a serious lingering question. Was all this a signal that I should have continued on into medicine? No one could answer that, but a consensus of advice was that it was now a time to finish the flying assignment. Medicine could wait.

I returned to a completely new arrangement. Our flying headquarters had been moved to a former cadet training field, Avenger Field in Sweetwater, Texas. It was a going concern. There were barracks, six to a unit, a regular mess hall, an HQ building, and even a complete infirmary. There were also black widow spiders, tarantulas, and scorpions.

I was assigned to a unit with Helen Dettweiler, a professional golf champion, Caryl Jones, a laboratory technician, a French girl Solange D'Hooghe, and Betty Greene, who planned to be a flying missionary in Africa some day. I was now in the fifth class.

However, I was not really in that class. I was nowhere. Instructors checked me off in the advanced planes, the North American AT-6 (the all–Air Force favorite) and the twin-engine Cessna C-78, then said, "To catch up and graduate with Class 5, you'll have to build up time. Report for night flying every night."

No one had more night flying than I did.

I used to report to the flight line early, to get my eyes used to the dark. Sitting by myself, I watched the lights, white and red, that were airplanes circling above the field. There were four quadrants and three layers of planes in each quadrant. You circled in your assigned quadrant until told to either change your altitude or come in to land. You had to keep reminding yourself that the moving lights were moving airplanes. And you could not slip out of your altitude. If there was no moon, it was like buzzing around in a dark pocket filled with airplanes that looked like flimsy lights.

We would take one night cross-country flight with our instructor, following the light beacons across Texas, like the early mail pilots.

We took off at dusk, when it was just dark enough to require the navigation lights on the wings and tail of our twin-engine advanced trainer, the Cessna C-78. Yet, we rose from semidarkness into still-sunlit sky. While we could still see our instruments clearly, we turned to our course of about 235 degrees for Midland, Texas, 100 miles to the southwest.

We were traveling three to a plane, two women pilots and an instructor. One woman would fly out, the other return; one would have the takeoff, the other the landing. We drew straws to see who would be first up. The instructor sat in the right-hand copilot seat. As we were not to have a solo night cross-country flight, his instructions would be telling.

Each of us had plotted the course and time of the flight, drawn a line on the chart, listed on our clipboards the checkpoints—the small towns of Roscoe, Loraine, Colorado City, Westbrook, Big Spring, Stanton, Paul, and Midland—plus the mileages and times between them. And we had checked the weather; we would have a tailwind out. The Texas-Pacific Railroad along the way would help, though not as much at night as in the daylight. Besides the lights of each town, blinking beacons, like navigational buoys for ships, would guide us. Modern radio navigation (Omni, LORAN, GPS) has made these comforting beacons obsolete, and even in 1943 radio ranges were already in use.

As the silent blue shadow of night spread over the land from the east, we, too, were finally encompassed in darkness. We flew on in silence at 3,000 feet, the cockpit dark, only the instrument dials lit, and, if we spoke, our voices seemed disembodied. This was instrument flying, in that we monitored the attitude of the airplane through airspeed, altitude, and turn and bank instrument readings, as we could no longer depend on visually checking the horizon.

"Too bad we have no moon."

"Hope you brought a small flashlight in order to check your chart," the instructor said. We hadn't.

"Then you've memorized your list of checkpoints?" More or less.

"Tune in the radio range. You should be riding in the A-signal quadrant," he continued. (The radio range was set up so A-signals [.-] and N-signals [-.] overlap into a steady signal when you are "on the beam.")

"Watch your altitude. You've lost nearly 100 feet."

And so it went, as we bore through the night sky, skipping along the beacons, listening to the radio range, and watching our altitude and speed. We did not, as did some, engage in aerobatics and other games along the way.

On our return, about two hours after our takeoff, we called in by radio for instructions for landing. As we approached we could see the beehive of lights still circling above the airport.

"C-78 Eight Zero, cleared to land on Runway 9, on straight-in approach."

There was an extra bonus in this night flying. Flying in the twin-engine, five-passenger C-78, we flew, for the first time, with one another. And it was impressive to see what good pilots our fellow students had become.

CHAPTER 7

Deaths

One morning we awoke to our first deaths—two women pilots and an instructor lost on a night cross-country flight. We never were told exactly what happened. Perhaps no one knew. The plane had crashed and burned, or perhaps it was in the opposite order.

The two women, Margaret Seip and Helen Severson, were best friends of Caryl Jones in my barracks. Caryl may have learned the details, but she did not talk about it, preferring to mourn in silence while she kept busy collecting together her friends' things to send to the families. The rest of us were saddened and sobered by their loss, by their absence. It forced us to look within and face our own mortality.

Up to now, we had focused on flying well, and those things we did not do well—landings, steep turns, holding altitude, or whatever—we simply practiced until they were right. We had confidence in our skills. But the actuality of death we had not faced. Now it suddenly hovered there in front of us. We could fail. We could die. Yet, we secretly felt "it won't happen to me." If we did not feel that, we could simply dissolve in terror, we would take off with a dry mouth, every strange noise would indicate a bad engine. But Fleischman's challenge to "take it" strengthened us. And wasn't the way we faced death in the skies exactly what Cochran had tried to foretell in our interview? Many of the women turned to their God—who, for them, was indeed their "copilot."

Our instructors, with a double care—for themselves and for their students—kept us out there flying. There was new emphasis on attention to safety, but they also watched to see that a student did not become overly concerned with detail and nervous. For there would be other deaths, but also other successful grapplings with death. One student, for example, Lorraine Rodgers, solo in a BT-13, with some sort of control failure, found herself on her back with no control, low to the ground. Somehow, she got herself out of the cockpit and her parachute open. (At first, she was told by her commanding officer that it was impossible to get out of a BT-13 on its back, and she was blamed for leaving it. An investigation exonerated her, however.)

Finally, our training came to an end. The hours in each airplane were finished. Our class, 43-W-5, had 55 hours in the primary PT-19, in the basic BT-13, 65 hours, and in the advanced AT-6 and twin-engine C-78, 60 hours. We had 38 hours of instrument flying, some of which were in the airplane simulator, the Link trainer. For other classes, the arrangement of hours differed slightly. Also, our ground school tests in navigation, meteorology, aircraft engines, and Morse code were over. The final evaluations of us as pilots were made. Some would be disappointed and would not pass.

The evaluation was not merely a summary of numbers or percentage points. We could only guess what it included in order to come to a final judgment of adequacy or failure. It seemed as though we were judged on the very way we walked, moved, and thought, and was the difference between being "in charge" and being "too cocky," or being hesitant and nervous or confident and at home in the aircraft. But for all of us, there was always the dread of proving inadequate. Those who failed were called "washouts." The washout rate per class was said to be slightly lower than that of the male cadets.

September 11, 1943, was graduation day for class 43-W-5. Of 127 trainees, 85 graduated. The day was clear and sunny and this class (except for me) was the first to have had all its training at Sweetwater Avenger Field. (Here it was the 318th WFTD rather than the 319th.)

We slicked up our khakis and overseas caps (no uniform yet, but coming) for the graduation ceremonies. Behind an honor guard carrying the American flag, we marched across the field two by two to the accompaniment of the Big Spring Bombardier School Band, and lined up before the receiving stand and honored guests. These included Jacqueline Cochran, Director of Women Pilots AAF, and Ethel Sheehy, Chief Recruiting Officer, with Brig. Gen. Isaiah Davies, Commanding General of the 34th Flying Training Wing, as guest speaker. We stood in the sun during the speeches, and then passed the dignitaries, one by one, to receive our silver wings from Jackie Cochran. General Davies welcomed us to our Air Force duty and wished us well in our future endeavors.

We did not throw our hats in the air after the ceremonies, nor did we squeal in excitement like high school graduates. What would come next was too serious.

Friends, hoping not to be separated, checked the assignment list with trepidation when it was posted. Each graduate was appointed to one of the Air Transport Command ferry bases, in Delaware, Michigan, Massachusetts, or

California. Although we had requested certain bases, not all found their requests met.

Two of us, Betty Greene and I, were assigned to the tow-target squadron of the Artillery Base at Camp Davis, N.C. We joined a WASP contingent, many from class 43-3, already there. We were to replace two women who had been killed in crashes that were to remain controversial.

Ultimately, the whole Camp Davis program became controversial. This was Cochran's first attempt at placing WASPs in other than ferrying jobs. She allegedly selected her top pilots from class 43-3 and later from class 43-4 (about twenty-four from each class) to prove that her pilots were professionals who could take on more dangerous jobs in the war effort. She promised the women that they would be flying bigger aircraft than they would in the ferry command, that this was a secret and crucial mission, and that their performance here would affect the future standing of women pilots.

Cochran was looking ahead to all sorts of other slots for "her" pilots, and this colored her handling of Camp Davis's desperate problems. Her main worry, it turned out, was that these problems be kept secret. She demanded secrecy from the pilots, and even went to the mechanics for a promise of secrecy. The basic problems here were, first, prejudice against the WASPs, and, second and probably more important, poor—nonexistent in some cases—aircraft maintenance.

The first accident even Cochran believed was sabotage. The plane's engine quit and it crashed on its back on the runway. On examination, it was found that the fuel had been laced with sugar, which had stopped the engine. Unbelievably, this was hushed up. Whether or not anyone was blamed or punished we never knew, even though others had also had engines quit.

In the second, even more terrible accident, the pilot could not get out of a crashed burning aircraft because the canopy latch would not open. The plane's log—or "Form 1"—showed that this complaint had been written up but was never repaired. It seemed that a habit had been formed to "red line" the Form 1 if some rather small problem was at stake; that is, simply record what was wrong, but let it fly.

When Cochran came down from Washington after each accident, the women confronted her. She promised to look into everything but, in the end, flew back to Washington with no further discussion. Two women resigned in disgust—or fear. (Being Civil Service employees, we *could* resign.)

Yet, in spite of all this, the women tried to make the best of it, tried to serve the Air Force loyally. But they learned that to stay alive they would have to look out for themselves. They began to check the airplanes they were to fly themselves, and they befriended the mechanics, who were suffering with "combat reject" aircraft and a lack of parts to keep them going.

Innocently, Betty and I walked into this hornet's nest, believing that we were, as the others had thought, specially selected. Our first test was to acclimate ourselves to our bare barracks rooms so recently occupied by women like ourselves, but now dead.

There was certainly no welcome here for WASPs. A men's squadron was already in place, needing, they thought, no help from us. They did appreciate being released to better jobs elsewhere, however. The commanding officer did not even try to hide his annoyance at having us foisted upon him.

The camp itself was a makeshift, temporary base. Simple wooden buildings and tents stood in the sand in rows, without the softness of trees or grass. They were crowded together as if to protect one another from the encircling Great Dismal Swamp of North Carolina. Any plane downed in it would sink out of sight in a day, and a pilot would have to extract himself from the jungle ooze and resident snakes and bobcats.

The airport was a single narrow runway at the edge of the buildings. Along it stood the planes, all of them painted olive drab, showing that they had been retired from combat.

There was plenty of flying for everyone, as it turned out. There was even an interesting variety of missions to fly in several different types of aircraft, though never the big aircraft promised in Cochran's grandiose presentation.

We started off flying a treetop-level pattern over the camp to test artillery tracking. For this, we flew the small L-5, a Cub-type airplane, back and forth and round and round for several hours. Next, we took four-hour stretches at 10,000 feet (as high as you should go without oxygen) in the A-24, the Douglas Dauntless two-seater, single-engine dive-bomber. We flew solo back and forth to test radar tracking by the gunner trainees. The seat got pretty hard after four hours, and it was rumored that long exposure to radar made you sterile.

We towed a ragged cloth sleeve target behind a Lockheed B-34, a twin-engine bomber similar to Amelia Earhart's Electra, out over the ocean for the gunners to practice shooting. It was a surprise to realize that the queer round blobs of smoke outside the window were live ammunition exploding a bit ahead of the target! Some airplanes came back with bullet holes in them.

At night, we flew searchlight missions. That is, we flew a racetrack pattern at different altitudes, which the artillery men tried to follow with their searchlights. This was essentially instrument flying. If you looked outside at the light, you lost your night vision and could not even read the instruments.

Finally, we started experimenting with robot drone planes, flying them by radio control from a mother ship. The bright-red drones were flown by servo controls much the way model radio-controlled airplanes are flown from the ground. They were flown from the twin-engine C-78, one woman flying the C-78, another "flying" the drone.

The towing and searchlight missions were flown with the men pilots. The favorite women pilots got to fly with the better men pilots. And these favorites went out on dates with their pilots. They became those pilots' "girls." Even if you were one of the chosen, you felt it was another demoralizing process, along with the dismal environment, lack of welcome, and personal danger.

The varied flying and the building up of flying time and experience were the pluses in the assignment. And there was one more perk. In any free moment from target flying, we were urged to take an aircraft on a cross-country flight, simply to exercise our cross-country skills (or possibly, just to get us out of sight for a while).

Sometimes we would go off three or four at a time, practicing (loose) formation flying on the way. Once, we flew to Kitty Hawk, landing at Mateo Island on the short aircraft carrier simulation runway. When we slid back our canopies, unbuckled, and climbed out of our Curtiss A-25 dive-bombers—bigger and faster than the A-24s—the linesmen coming out to check us in suddenly stopped.

"Girls!" they shouted. "And what can we do for you ladies?"

What a pleasant change from the Camp Davis "welcome."

"We'd like some fuel, please. And a look at your base here. Is this really where the Navy pilots practice carrier landings?"

"Yes, indeed," said one. "So you can consider yourselves carrier pilots now!"

Then we had to explain who we were. I don't know why they believed us, in our two-sizes-too-big flying overalls. When we signed in at the office, the officer in charge was equally amazed.

"Those are Navy SB2Cs, aren't they. How come?"

We told him they were Air Force versions without the folding wings the Navy needed.

"Come back again," they shouted, as we climbed back into our "carrier" planes.

On another outing, solo, returning to the field, I flew all the way at treetop level, following the contour of hills and valleys, over barns and animals in their fields. I was going about 180 miles an hour, but it felt like 300. (A foolish and illegal performance.)

Another day, my A-24, though it looked fine on pre-takeoff checks, coughed and then quit on takeoff. I had passed the first third of the runway and had several hundred feet of altitude. Although I was losing altitude, it would not be enough to get back on the runway. The swamp lay beyond. I tried to squeeze speed and altitude out of it by pulling up the nose, then letting it down before it stalled. It seemed to work. I touched down just before the end of the runway, braked, and turned into the taxi strip.

Again, I had been lucky on a dead-stick landing.

"Don't attempt to fly that airplane," I heard from the control tower. "Leave it right there." I did.

Duty at Camp Davis had few carefree interludes. Indeed, in many ways it was grim. But it showed the cool courage and dedication of WASPs in their service in the Air Force that they faced the difficulties and dangers here without help from Commanding Officer Stephenson or Cochran or Washington, and took upon themselves the task of protecting themselves as best they could. Without complaints, they continued to fly missions for artillery men who were only just learning how to shoot their guns.

I felt honored to fly with them. Among them were former classmates from 43-W-3: Lois Hollingsworth, Kay Menges, Jean Pearson, Frances Grimes, Dora Dougherty, and Mary Lee Leatherbee.

Cochran had warned us that in our WASP duties there would be risks and dangers and that no special quarter would be given the women pilots, but we were not ready for the fact that being only Civil Service employees meant that there was no Air Force money to pay for funerals or transportation of "remains"-laden coffins. We had to pass the hat for contributions for that—and for an American flag to accompany them, too.

CHAPTER 8

New Horizons

Sometimes you attune yourself to simply living one day at a time, trying to make the best of it when, if you concentrated on the future, the outlook would look only bleak. Then, suddenly, for no apparent reason, there comes a complete change, a shift that will change a life forever.

So it was one windy February day in 1944 at Camp Davis. With the sand blowing about the barracks as usual, and the same bustle of pilots off meeting their appointments on the flight line, there were two new assignments for Betty Greene and me. We were to report immediately to Wright Field in Dayton, Ohio, for temporary duty where we would test high-altitude and low-temperature equipment proposed for the WASPs.

It didn't sound like much at first. No mention of flying.

We reported (using commercial airline) to Col. Randolph Lovelace, director of the Aeromedical Laboratory at Wright Field. He was expecting us and welcomed us.

He took us to a big window overlooking the field.

"First, you must realize what Wright Field is," he said. "You can see the runways. Grouped around them and up on this hill are laboratories—for powerplant studies, for propellers, for electronics, for static testing, and so on. Even before Pearl Harbor this was the largest and most important testing center in the world for Air Force aircraft, and for some foreign aircraft as well. The Wright Field adjunct at Muroc Dry Lake in California and government laboratory at NACA in Langley, Virginia, add to the research facilities.

"At Aeromed Lab, we are studying how flying these fighting aircraft affects the pilots flying them. We are studying especially high-altitude flying and the effects of oxygen deprivation, and the stress on the body of gravity (G forces) in acceleration, in dive recovery and fast turns, and how we can alleviate those effects."

We looked farther off and saw many hangars and the laboratories above the field. None were temporary wooden buildings.

"What is that loud noise that seems constant?" we asked.

"That comes from the wind tunnels, where aircraft models are undergoing speed, stability, and compressibility testing. And you are right. It is a constant noise here!"

He took us into his office.

"I'm going to turn you over to Major McCardle. He is a doctor who has specialized in high-altitude medicine and he is in charge of the pressure chamber. He will take you up to simulated altitude in the chamber to show you the effects of oxygen deprivation before you take your flight in our special high-altitude B-17 to test the proposed equipment for the WASPs. And I want you to meet some of the other experts here. You'll be here a week or so.

"Oh, you have another job to do here—to design a relief tube for women. Planes now have only male equipment. You'll talk that over with Major McCardle and with Brad Washburn, whose expertise is in mountain expeditions. He was first to climb Mount McKinley in Alaska, our highest mountain. If you can decide on a proper design, we'll have a model made and you will have to test it yourselves!"

The colonel made a quick call to Major McCardle, who soon appeared and took us to lunch. We sat at a table with bright and talkative medical experts in a large hall with vaulted ceilings.

We listened, and spoke only when asked questions—mostly about what in the world WASPs were, and what our backgrounds were. McCardle leaned beyond an ex-professor from MIT beside him.

"I'll take you down to the pressure chamber after lunch," he said. He was tall and slim and soft-spoken. "Then you'll be ready for your flight test in the B-17 tomorrow morning."

We wanted to hear more about the B-17 flight.

"You'll be testing the clothing and oxygen masks in the nose of the B-17," McCardle said. We found he didn't overdo explanations. We would have to keep asking questions.

"You'll be going up in a specially equipped B-17 to 43,000 feet—as high as it can go. And you'll be pretty well covered with thermocouples to record temperatures all over your bodies. Other Wright Field tests will be going on in this special B-17 at the same time."

Meanwhile, the conversation at the table went from discussions of oxygen levels in red blood cells to Ph.D. dissertations coming due.

"Which of you is Brad Washburn?" I ventured. "I understand he has climbed Mt. McKinley."

"He's not only climbed it. He is Mr. Mt. McKinley himself. He's working on experimental climbing gear here."

All eyes turned toward Brad Washburn, a slightly built man with brown eyes and greying hair. He was not embarrassed by the attention, and it was not hard to picture a far-sighted, steady mountain gaze. At the time, he was engrossed in some technical problems with his tests and avoided chit-chat about himself.

McCardle led us downstairs to this pressure chamber, a long, steel, tubular structure with several portholes and big control valves. He opened one of the pressurized doors, ushered us in, and closed the door. There was a steady hum.

"These pamphlets will tell you about the pressure chamber and why it is a necessary tool," he said, handing us the pamphlets, and a piece of paper and a pencil.

The pamphlets showed its construction and how, by changing the pressure and oxygen content inside, it could simulate different levels of the atmosphere.

"We can take you up to 25,000 feet as we decompress at the same rate as the true atmosphere does, and at the same time lower the temperature so you can see why you can't simply fly to any altitude you want. I want you to write your name and address and the date on that piece of paper—right now."

We wrote as the machine continued to hum. Every now and then a face would appear at one of the portholes. A dial on the wall showed our changing altitude.

A little while later, McCardle asked us to write our name and address and date.

"You're at 10,000 feet simulated atmosphere," he said. "How does your writing look?"

It didn't look too bad, we said. The machine hummed on.

"As we go higher, I'll watch you carefully for signs of oxygen deprivation, and I'll take a blood sample. Now write your name and so on again. You are now at 20,000 feet, and we'll stay here momentarily."

We didn't think our writing looked bad, and we felt perfectly all right.

"We'll go down now, and examine your writing." The machine hummed differently, and the temperature rose.

"Look at your high-altitude work," McCardle said.

It was sloppy. In fact, mine had no numbers at all. And yet we had felt fine and thought our performance was good.

"Exactly," said McCardle. "That's the danger. You don't realize you have oxygen deprivation and think you can handle anything, but the next thing, if we had stayed at altitude, you'd have passed out. So remember, you must use oxygen beginning at 10,000 feet, even if, or rather especially if, you think you don't need it."

We pondered the tell-tale writing exercises.

"We're finding now that at 45,000 feet, even with 100 percent oxygen, we must provide pressure, either in the delivery of the oxygen or by using a pressurized cabin—but you don't need to worry about that now." (Much later, however, I would test pressurization in an experimental P-47 at altitude.)

Next morning, Dr. Alice Brues prepared us for our B-17 flight. We were covered with thermocouples that would record our body temperature more or less all over. They were disks at the end of wires and were stuck on with some sort of goo, so we had to move carefully. Then we were dressed in the heavy-weather clothing we were to test, and supplied with (and shown how to use) oxygen masks.

Dr. Brues's test program turned out to be very extensive—over a week long, flying every day in different planes, wearing a variety of cold-weather gear. If we hadn't been more interested in simply flying planes, we might have appreciated her thoroughness.

The tests, Dr. Brues's final report dated March 4, 1944, says, were to determine "the best possible flying outfit—including suit, gloves, boots and helmet—for constant wear for at least three hours' duration at or about 0°C." Actually the temperature ranged from −14°C. to 0°C. The clothing included medium-sized Air Force men's clothing, J. Cochran–designed clothes, clothes designed by Dr. Brues, by Willis and Geiger Co. in New York, and by Oldin Dennis Co. in New York.

Our first day of tests would be the high-altitude test in the B-17. We clambered into the nose of the B-17 in our bulky clothes and crouched on the floor. It was hard to see out. We just guessed when we were about to take off and when we had finished climbing to our altitude—at 43,000 feet certainly the highest we had ever been.

As we climbed, we saw ice crystals forming on the windows and around our feet. We were plugged into the 100 percent oxygen system, and remained more or less warm. We tried to imagine how a gunner in this compartment would have to learn to handle this confined space, his heavy clothing, oxygen mask, and gun.

Dr. Brues informed us when we reached altitude (as I remember we never reached 43,000 feet exactly, but it was over 35,000) and questioned us to see how cold we were, and where. Betty and I had different clothes on, which were to be compared to see which was best. We had to answer questions, for example, on whether the three-fingered glove designed by Dr. Brues was warmer and more flexible than the Cochran glove, whether we stayed warm in our suits or did we have to move about to keep warm (yes, we moved about, flexed our fingers, wiggled our toes to keep warm).

The next day, we moved to single-engine aircraft (we flew each other) to test the warmth with wind. The canopy was left open varying amounts. Results of these tests showed alpaca was too bulky, hydrolyzed interlining was better. Boots that zipped all the way down were best. Even underwear was compared, and socks. According to the March 4 report, we flew each other in "cold windy cockpits" of A-24 and A-25 dive-bombers and in the AT-6 trainer for two and a half hours between 2,500- and 10,000-foot altitudes and through "all the actions required in piloting a plane." We tested boots by walking in the mud and then climbing on the wings of the planes to see if traction was good, and whether they slipped on a wet wing. The tests even considered the flexibility of the knee, the number of zippers and pockets on the legs of the trousers, and whether the trouser leg stayed in the boot when the knee was bent during flying operations.

The winners were the Oldin Dennis suit, the Hood Rubber Co. boot of WASP design, the WASP design gloves (similar to Air Force design), and the regulation Air Force helmet.

Then it was time to talk about the women's relief tube. We discussed with Dr. Brues anatomy, positions, fit, and how it would connect with the male relief tube (a discussion that might have been delicate with a male technician). Possibly, each woman pilot would have her own utensil (packed in a nice leather case perhaps). We actually settled on a workable design. Dr. Brues's report describes it this way: "Relief tube is small bowl-shaped funnel that will fit in the palm of the hand and will thus be placed in position for use."

But there were other problems—the main one was access. We decided on a crotch zipper in the flying suit or coveralls. But this would require other crotch zippers in trousers underneath, and then in the underwear. (Nevertheless, I would test this contraption much later, and under not ideal conditions.)

As we sat around a big table, discussing these problems, however, we could hear outside, beyond the walls of the lab, bombers and fighters taking off, the bombers fairly shaking the building. As interesting as the Aeromed Lab was, it was those airplanes that interested us more.

We talked it over later and decided we would like to transfer to this fascinating place, the actual center of the Air Force.

"It might not be impossible," Colonel Lovelace told us. "Why don't you try? I'd be glad to make an appointment for you to see the chief of the Flight Test Division, Col. Ernest Warburton."

That afternoon, we walked down from the Aeromed Lab to the control tower and the administration building where Colonel Warburton had his office. We passed the fighters (P-47s, P-51s, P-38s, P-39s, P-63s, a P-40, a

German Me-109, and a Spitfire) lined up in front of the Fighter Flight Test Branch hangar. Beyond them were the bombers in front of their hangar (B-17s, B-24s, B-25s, B-26s, an A-26, British Mosquito and Lancaster bombers, and a German Ju-88). Across the taxistrip were the transports (C-47, C-45, and helicopters). In front of the administration building was an assortment of civilian aircraft.

Aircraft were taking off and landing, and in the background was the ubiquitous roar of the wind tunnels.

Colonel Warburton and his second-in-command, Lt. Col. Osmond Ritland, welcomed us formally and motioned us to chairs. (We, fortunately, had on our new Air Force blue uniforms and hats.)

"Colonel Lovelace says you rather like this place," Colonel Warburton said with a smile. Both he and Colonel Ritland were ex-combat test pilots and looked the part—erect, tanned, direct, and with what pilots are wont to call the gaze of eagles. Colonel Warburton was dark-haired and rather stern, Colonel Ritland almost a redhead and quietly amused.

"We assume you are serious in your request to transfer," Colonel Warburton continued. "And we would like to have you here, on one condition. That you first act as assistant operations officers until you prove your seriousness. After that, we'll talk about what flying you will do. One will go to Fighter Test, the one with the most flying time [I raised my hand], and the other to Transport. We have a WAAC captain as operations officer at Bomber Test. Now, is that acceptable?"

We would have scrubbed floors to be assigned there.

"Yes, indeed," we said.

"I can't promise that your transfer will go through. But I'll certainly try."

Back at Camp Davis, we anxiously awaited word from Wright Field. We flew our tow-target missions carefully, checking the airplanes well beforehand. We didn't really believe our transfers would be forthcoming. Why would they need us there after all? And we hadn't complained about or asked for refuge from Camp Davis. Perhaps they really needed operations officers and held out a flying possibility as a lure. We did think we had cooperated well on the clothing tests, but we weren't interested in a clothing-testing career. We hoped those tests were over.

The only possible reasons for our transfers would have to be that (1) operations officers were needed at Wright Field Test Division and (2) that Cochran would be glad to have WASPs in still another type of duty, especially if it took us away from troubled Camp Davis. Requests for change of base, if allowed at all, usually were not granted until after six months at a base. We would be shy one month of that.

Before two weeks were up, our kind—and patient—supervisor, Jean Forster, called us into her office. "You two are to be transferred permanently to Wright Field," she said. "I guess you did well testing the clothing."

"Do we just go back to Aeromed Lab, then?" What a disappointment.

Jean opened the orders and read them again.

"To the Materiel Command," she read. "Reporting to Colonel Ernest Warburton, Chief of Flight Test Division." This was the time to throw our hats in the air! Suddenly it seemed a window opened wide, and the sun was pouring in. We did it!

In the end Betty Greene decided to stay with her friends in the WASP detachment at Camp Davis. I was assigned to Fighter Flight Test Branch (FFT), reporting there in early March 1944. I was not to see another WASP until long after the WASPs were disbanded. It was not until later that I learned that Camp Davis was finally given up as a WASP base on March 21, 1944, and its WASPs sent to Otis Field in Massachusetts and Liberty Field in Georgia, for a much happier time.

For me, I could not imagine what lay ahead. But, if I could prove my "seriousness," I might become the only female experimental test pilot of military combat planes at Wright Field in World War II.

As for the war, by the spring of 1944 there was some encouraging news—the Allies had recaptured the Solomon and Marshall Islands and in Europe 800 B-17 Flying Fortresses had dropped 2,000 bombs on Berlin—but the end still looked far away. And the cross-Channel invasion still had to be made.

CHAPTER 9

The Test Pilots

"They know you are coming," Colonel Ritland said quietly.

As he turned the doorknob, the conversation behind it stopped. The door opened upon a tableau of men in Air Force uniform, some standing, some sitting, in forced casualness. I saw curiosity, interest, and friendliness, no smugness, no coarseness.

"This is the WASP, which stands for Women Airforce Service Pilots, who has been assigned to FFT," Colonel Ritland said. "She'll be helping at the operations desk and learning what we do here, and how we do it."

I hoped my pilot's wings spoke loudly enough that I would be doing some flying, too.

"I'll turn you over to Major Petrie, FFT chief, for introductions and explanations. Good luck, Ann," meaning the unsaid, "You are on your own now."

As Colonel Ritland left, Maj. Chris Petrie, stocky, sandy-haired, blue-eyed, smiling, stepped forward and shook hands.

"Welcome to Fighter Flight Test Branch. It'll be a little overwhelming at first, but we'll help you get acclimated. First, this is Capt. Darrell Sims. You'll be helping him on operations. It's the best place to learn what goes on."

Captain Sims nodded, not quite smiling. I hoped he realized I was really going to be helping him, not taking his job.

Major Petrie then introduced the rest, about ten pilots. Throughout the next few days I learned something of their stories and personalities. But for that first day, Captain Sims had the detail of showing me around—the office, the ready room, the flight line, the hangar and maintenance department, and of course, the operations desk. There would be a slight problem in the "ready" room—where pilots get ready to fly.

"We'll assign you a locker here," Sims was saying. "Let's see, I guess we'll have to get a signal for when you are changing into flying clothes."

We both laughed.

"But anyhow, you put your parachute and flying coveralls in here, and your uniform while you are flying—when you fly," he added cautiously.

On the operations desk was a large chart, divided into squares, with the pilots' names on the left, the times of day across, with a special column for the aircraft and test assignments. The whole introductory survey took most of the day, as Sims also had to man the desk. The requirements there, I found out about next day.

For the night, I would share an apartment in Dayton with WAAC Capt. Jane Arbogust, operations officer at Bomber Flight Test (BFT). Transportation to and from the field would be shared, a different Test Section person driving each day. So much for the bare-bones logistics.

I met Captain Arbogust at the apartment. She was both brusque and brisk. Irish, short, with green eyes, she took charge. The apartment had two bedrooms, one large, one small. Arbogust's was the large one. We would take turns supplying food and cleaning the place, one week at a time. No males would be entertained there. It was on the second floor and looked out on an alley. Arbogust was the most interesting part of the apartment. We got along fine right off.

Next morning I reported to Captain Sims, who gave me a list of the airplanes to be used that day. I then walked out to the maintenance hangar and checked them with Captain Kuhn, the maintenance chief.

"The ones that are out front on the line are the ones ready to go," he would tell me each morning, but Sims wanted a signed okay releasing them. Those not ready were similarly noted in writing. Besides being free of any maintenance problems, they had to be full of fuel, oxygen, hydraulic fluid, coolant, and, often, ordnance (ammunition). Further, being test airplanes, they were equipped with black boxes —barograph, cameras, and intricate instrumentation—to record the aircraft's performance. Though this was before computers, instrumentation was beginning to back up the pilot's evaluation. Aircraft testing was becoming a science, I learned.

The test pilots looked over Sims's shoulder at the chart to see whether their planes were ready, if their tests were continuing. They milled around, like racehorses anxious to start the race. Outside, planes were starting up. As they turned across the door, their slipstreams sent wind and dust inside.

Sims okayed each flight and checked off each pilot, giving him a release slip to give the linesman as he left.

"Never let a pilot go without this release slip," Sims warned, like a mother hen. "Some of them with current tests see their aircraft on the line and want to go right off and fly, so you have to be careful."

"What are they all testing?" I asked Sims. "Most of those planes have been in use by the Air Force a long time."

"First, you have to realize that planes here are being evaluated for acceptance by the Air Force. If a company puts out a new model, it has to be evaluated from the standpoint of whether or not it actually performs as advertised, so to speak. Then there are new fuels, which may add or subtract power, and so on. Then there are airplanes like the XP-39E [a new model of the Bell P-39] for performance or engine tests. The P-39 has a flat spin, for instance, so we are to figure out why and how to fix it. Then, our aircrafts' performance is compared with the foreign planes."

"A lot different from the movie version of a test pilot's work."

"Yes."

"What exactly do you mean by performance?"

"Well, are its performance factors as stated by the manufacturer? Are its low and high speeds reached by the power settings given? The altitude reached by the rate of climb given? More than that and more basic, how stable is the aircraft? If you release your controls, does it come back to level flight? Not all fighters do. If you put it in a bank, does it go on rolling—that's static instability—or does it tend to stay in that bank or return to level flight? Down at NACA [National Advisory Committee for Aeronautics] at Langley Field [Virginia], Dr. Robert Gilruth has developed these stability and control criteria."

"My, it's complicated."

"It gets more complicated. All the labs on the hill have little gimmicks to add and to try out. Better propellers, heat exchangers, hydraulic pumps. Different landing gear, and so on. But we have entirely new and experimental aircraft here, too. And we have a few new flight problems. Compressibility is one. That's what happens at the sound barrier. When the aircraft reaches the speed of sound [about 700 MPH at 60°F at sea level, lowering with higher altitude] it's a rough ride, and control forces change. Then there is the pressure oxygen barrier."

"Yes, I heard about that one at the Aeromed Lab."

"The point of all the testing, you see, is to make our Air Force planes not only faster and so on, but also safer and easier to fly for the pilots who will fly them in combat," Sims said.

When the operations desk quieted a bit, and most of the pilots were off flying, I asked Sims something about himself.

"I don't see you on this flight list for today."

Sims looked off into the distance, as if he was looking for a plane outside, or maybe a bird. "No," he said quietly.

I felt I had asked the wrong question.

"No," he said again. "I've had my share of flying. . . . I was a bomber pilot—B-24s—stationed in England. I flew on the Ploesti oil raids, more flights than I needed to. That was enough. Oh, sometimes I go up for a little spin."

He smiled and was ready to go to another subject. I never questioned him about it again. I did learn that he came from a small town in Wyoming, but not much else.

The pilots began to return from their flights. Maj. Fred Borsodi (Sims reminded me of their names) came in carrying a black box (a barograph), cap pushed back, oxygen mask dangling.

He was second in command, Sims said. An ex-combat pilot in North Africa, he had captured a German Ju-88 bomber and flown it back to the United States. Before that, he had been to Yale and had been an Indy 500 driver. Balding, freckled, and smiling, he was full of enthusiasm, not only about flying but about anything he happened to be talking about. He was married and had two little girls.

I looked at the sheet and saw that he'd been flying a P-51 that morning on compressibility dive tests.

"Is Sims getting you to do all his work?" he asked.

"I'm telling her what real test pilots do."

"Don't believe it. They just go up and fly around."

Capt. Dick Johnston came in next. He quietly signed in, and asked if Sims was taking good care of me. I saw that he'd been flying accelerated service performance tests on a late model P-47.

"He's testing performance with a new fuel and with water injection," Sims said. "He's a Southerner."

Captains Zed Fountain and M. L. Smith signed in.

"They're Southerners, too," Sims said. "They like coon hunting. Ask them about coon hunting at night."

Fountain had been flying a P-47 and Smith a P-63. Both of them had flown combat at Guadalcanal, as had Johnston.

Then with a burst Maj. Perry Ritchie pushed through the door. He was just finishing a Hershey chocolate bar. He'd been doing high-speed dive tests in a P-47 (he'd already had to jump from one, Sims said). And he looked like the stereotype of a test pilot—tall, blond, all-American country boy. But he was also an aeronautical engineer and had contributed much knowledge to aircraft testing, Sims said later. As a matter of fact, several of the pilots were aeronautical engineers, and most were ex-combat pilots. Yet, here they were, do-

ing dangerous experimental testing. I was standing among the cream of the
Air Force, surely. About half of them were married, with small children, living off the field in Dayton.

There was one more important pilot—Maj. Gustav Lundquist. He had also
been doing compressibility tests. He was a spit-and-polish Nordic blond and
was, Sims said, one of the most particular of the pilots, but he felt deficient as
he'd had no combat. Whenever he requested a transfer, it was denied. He was
already too good a test pilot. He was needed here.

There were others, Sims said, and one more was out at Muroc Air Force
Base in the California desert, where the more secret or intractable tests were
beginning to be run. Maj. Wally Lien was there flying an experimental jet
fighter, our first jet, the Bell XP-59A.

Then, as an afterthought, Sims added that the real chief of FFT was a mysterious Lt. Col. Harney Estes, who was temporarily in England. I did not pay
much attention to that at the time. Just another Air Force officer, I thought.

These men were basically very diverse, yet in the Air Force context they
looked at life in the same way, spoke the same language, faced the same fact of
their mortality in this particular assignment in their wartime service. They
seemed too mature and self-confident—or fatalistic—for any petty jealousies.
It was simply taken for granted that Borsodi and Lundquist were the best and
were assigned the most difficult or exacting tests. Ritchie also held a special
position in the group. He was a native of Dayton, a pilot full of exuberance
who pushed his testing to the very limits of speed—and of safety.

But there was one proud allegiance they all subscribed to—they were
fighter pilots, and all those words implied. They flew alone in the wide sky,
faced alone the challenges of their tests, their balking engines, their fear of in-
adequacy against the powerful forces purposely released in the quest for aircraft performance data.

Although these pilots were still in their early 20s, as I was, I felt in awe of
them and what they had done, what they knew about aircraft and about flying
them. I did not feel like pushing myself ahead here. I felt my lack of experience
strongly and was determined to be helpful, as I tried to learn to be a test pilot.

I was amazed at their kindness and acceptance of me. I guess they knew I
would be no threat to them. In fact, they always treated me rather like a kid
sister, who wanted to play their games and appreciated how hard it was to excel at them. They encouraged me to aim for flying the fighters. They thought
it perfectly okay to tease me about my flying, but, in fact, they reassured me
that they wouldn't tease if they thought I wasn't up to it.

They asked about the WASPs—how many? Why?—Our training? And
about the target towing for Camp Davis artillery men.

"Not one of the Air Force's nicest assignments!" they agreed.

"We're not in the Air Force actually. Just Civil Service now," I said. "But Cochran and General Arnold are working to get Congress to authorize our militarization. Right now, people on the street don't know what we are. They ask if we're bus drivers or police or what!"

"Well, looks like Warburton and Ritland think you're authentic." And they wanted to know how I had got the assignment to Wright Field. I could tell them how, but not exactly why. For whatever reason, I was more than grateful.

Every day I had more questions for Sims.

"I see there are quite a few compressibility tests. Explain more about that," I said.

"Well, you know from physics that water is not compressible, but air is— until an aircraft passing through it reaches the speed of sound, that is. Now, picture a plane flying along in the air at slow speeds. It gives advance notice, as it were, to the air ahead. As the plane speeds up, it gives less and less advance notice, until it reaches the speed of sound [between 600 and 700 MPH, depending on altitude and temperature]. Then, the plane meets air without advance notice and compresses the air at the sound barrier. With enough power and speed a plane could, we believe, break through it. But right now, when our fighters hit that barrier the plane can buffet and shake and the controls either lock or reverse. We've got to find out more about it."

Sims began to rummage through the drawer of his desk.

"I have the Gilruth report I spoke about here somewhere. You might read it overnight. It will give you a better idea of how intricately airplane flying characteristics are analyzed, as well as how they are being measured. Here it is."

"Thanks. I'll study it."

First off, Dr. Robert R. Gilruth, later awarded both the Collier Award and the presidential Medal of Freedom, became director of the NASA Space Center in Houston to run the Mercury, Gemini, and Apollo programs. The Collier Award, for the greatest advancement in aviation during the year, is aviation's highest award, and the Medal of Freedom is the highest civilian award. But Gilruth first made his name during World War II with his pioneering analysis and measurement of basic flight characteristics. The Air Force called upon him (and the NACA) for help on special problem airplanes—the B-24 and P-39 to mention two—and for special problems like compressibility at the sound barrier.

It was on the basis of his understanding and thoroughness that he was chosen to take us into space. Unfortunately, later, during the "space era," a sense of rivalry between NASA and the Air Force arose.

In his ten-page report, dated 1941 and entitled "Requirements for Satisfactory Flying Qualities of Airplanes," Gilruth describes "the need for quantitative design criterions for describing those qualities of an airplane that make up satisfactory controllability, stability and handling characteristics . . ." and suggests a detailed test procedure and test equipment to measure "the characteristics on which flying qualities depend."

Up to this point, he notes, flying specifications were simply based on subjective descriptions by pilots. They might complain of "tail heaviness" or other controls they didn't like, but it was difficult for the airplane designer to know what to do to the aircraft to produce the flying qualities pilots wanted. With the Gilruth test program, engineers, pilots, and everyone involved in a test program could, for the first time, use a common language to describe and measure "what influence various design features had on observed flying qualities."

Along with this minute analysis, instrumentation of the aircraft had developed so that effects upon the control surfaces of the aircraft could be measured, not just described. This not only checked the airplane, but gave a record of how the test pilot flew the test as well!

Because the development of flight testing procedures is the central concern here, a look at the topics covered in this early report may be useful. Gilruth divided the report into three parts:

I.   Requirements for Longitudinal Stability and Control
   A. Characteristics of uncontrolled longitudinal motion
   B. Characteristics of elevator control in steady flight
   C. Characteristics of elevator control in accelerated flight
   D. Characteristics of elevator control in landing
   E. Characteristics of elevator control on takeoff
   F. Limits of trim tab change due to power and flaps
   G. Characteristics of longitudinal trimming device
II. Requirements for Lateral Stability and Control
   A. Characteristics of uncontrolled lateral and directional motion
   B. Aileron control characteristics
   C. Yaw due to ailerons
   D. Limits of rolling moment [measurement of an effect] due to sideslip
   E. Rudder control characteristics
   F. Yawing moment due to sideslip
   G. Pitching moment due to sideslip
   H. Crosswind force characteristics
   I. Characteristics of rudder and aileron trimming devices
III. Stalling Characteristics

Studying the report in depth gave me a view of what information the flight testing at Wright Field was after. Sims couldn't have given me a better introduction. I got the feeling that the aircraft was the patient, the test pilots the doctors examining its capabilities and deficiencies.

When I returned the report to Sims, he asked, "Have you read *Slide Rule* by Nevil Shute?"

"I've read some of his books. He was a British aeronautical engineer as well as a writer, wasn't he?"

"Yes, indeed. And he had his own company, too. *Slide Rule* addresses something you should know about if you are to understand how airplanes are made to go faster, other than just adding power. Something called boundary layer."

"I've heard the term. Tell me more."

"Shute describes crossing the Atlantic by dirigible, in the book. He was able to walk along the top of it while it was flying along at 110 MPH."

"Sounds like fun."

"The reason they could do that was, because of the shape and size of the dirigible, there was an eight-foot-thick boundary layer where the air simply rides along with the vehicle."

"Um-m."

"You've probably noticed how dirt will stay on the hood of your car no matter how fast you go. That's because of the boundary layer of air on the car's hood. This boundary layer caused by turbulence across the surface will slow the passage of air across a wing. Aeronautical engineers trying to increase an airplane's speed have been working to cut down that layer. First, they put a sleeve four feet wide over part of the wing to see if smoothing the area—cutting out struts, intakes, even screwholes—would make a difference. It did. Other studies were done on dolphins, unsuccessfully as it turned out, to try to see why they have no boundary layer along their skin to slow their passage through the water. Then they made the wings thinner and squared off the wingtips. These were tests done in the late thirties and early forties."

"Did they get rid of the boundary layer?"

"Enough to achieve smooth passage of air over the wing—the laminar flow airfoil, a great achievement—giving higher speed and lift."

I'd like to expand that answer of Sims's, briefly, with later knowledge of the laminar flow airfoil and its birth during the development of the P-51. My sources are, first, my husband, Bill Carl, an aeronautical engineer who served in the NACA during World War II, where some of the early airfoil tests and studies were done, and, second, aviation writer Peter Garrison, who has written fully on the subject.

In 1938, North American Aviation in California, headed by James H. "Dutch" Kindelberger, had designed and was building AT-6 trainers called Harvards for the British through the British Purchasing Commission in New York. Both the U.S. Navy and the U.S. Air Force used the AT-6 as well. In

1939, the company designed and built the B-25 bomber used in 1942 in Doolittle's raid on Tokyo. Then, in 1940, the British wanted a Curtiss P-40 fighter replacement. This would be the P-51, and would eventually be evaluated the best fighter of World War II. The British ordered 320 planes simply from the plans.

Among other innovations in the P-51 by Edgar Schmued, NAA chief designer, was this laminar flow airfoil. It evolved from wind-tunnel low-drag airfoil tests at NACA by aerodynamicist Russell Robinson that were further developed at NACA by Ed Horkey. These low-drag airfoil shapes were intended to "delay the onset of turbulence." Key to the airfoil shape was a smooth surface and a flat pressure distribution. To this end, Schmued had every rivet set flush with the aircraft's skin. With this smooth skin (plus the Rolls Royce Merlin engine) the P-51D (the model with the bubble canopy) could reach 490 MPH in level flight and a cruising range of 2,400 miles. The P-51 was, Garrison says, the first military aircraft to have this high-performance laminar flow airfoil wing. And he points out as well that "it was subsequently noticed that the laminar flow airfoils bore a strong resemblance to the cross-section of a trout!"

The P-51 was undergoing even further tests while I was at Wright Field (and afterward) in compressibility power dives.

My education in flight testing was now beginning. I looked forward to knowing more about the P-51. And, of course, I wanted to fly it.

Altitude
A test pilot does not think of sky
as the "firmament of heaven."
He thinks of it as a safety net below
or a target to reach above,
above, where the sky gets darker
and loses density,
where he begins to feel unstable
with no reference points or resistance,
like a plane on the end of a string,
where the horizon just begins to curve.
—Ann Carl

CHAPTER 10

I Fly

One morning a few weeks later Sims was on the phone as I came in.

"The telephone's for you," Sims said. "Colonel Ritland."

Had I failed to be "serious" enough? Was I being sent back to Camp Davis?

"Hello, Colonel Ritland."

"Sims says you are fitting into the routine there pretty well. So we think you should get out and fly a little. Sims will arrange it. And Administration may need you to fly some flights for them. But keep on the job at Operations, too."

"Sound okay?" Sims asked when I hung up. "By that smile, I guess 'yes.' You get the aircraft list from Kuhn and I'll dig up an airplane for you—a Piper Cub or something."

Later on, an AT-6, the good old North American single-engine advanced trainer, stood on the line, waiting. At the same time, it seemed, Major Ritchie came in.

"An AT-6!" Ritchie said. "My favorite airplane."

"Sorry, it's Ann's," Sims said with one of his searching-for-bird looks.

"When are you going up?" Ritchie asked. "Mind if I go along for the ride, maybe show you a few things?"

"Look out," Sims said.

So it was settled. We went out to the airplane. I climbed into the forward, pilot's seat in the cockpit, Ritchie behind.

"You go ahead and take it off and fly around. Then let me take it for a minute, then you land it. Forget I'm here. I'm just enjoying myself."

I took my first passenger at Wright Field off into the blue sky above Dayton. Only this wasn't *any* passenger. He was one of the best at FFT. He said to forget he was there.

The first thing was to locate myself so that I could bring him back to the right place. I saw Wright Field and its encircling buildings, and Vandalia Airport to the northwest, and Patterson Air Force Base to the northeast. The town of Dayton was in between. Surrounding Dayton was farmland. I'd better keep my toe on Dayton, I thought.

The AT-6 is a dancing airplane. It goes smoothly from a turn to the left to a turn to the right, from a climb to a glide. It is easy to forget a passenger as you swing into a chandelle turn or two or fly some lazy eights.

"Climb up and do some rolls. Then I'll do some," I suddenly heard in my earphones.

I climbed, did a snap roll or two, and a slow roll.

"It's yours," I said in the phones.

"Not too bad," he said, and did some quicker, better, and snappier. "Okay, take her in."

Every landing is a challenge. One never knows how it will go, even going through the same general procedure each time. This time I was lucky. We parked and climbed out.

"Thanks for the ride. Nice to just fly around once in a while. You're hoping to fly the fighters?"

"Hoping," I said.

"Keep at it," he said.

I never knew whether that was just a friendly flight or a check ride. But after that Administration called me to make flights for them, as Colonel Ritland said they would.

These administration flights were of many kinds, but all of them involved responsibility either for the plane or the passengers, sometimes for both.

I often flew generals to Bolling Field in Washington, D.C., in A-24s or A-25s, the single-engine dive-bombers. The first trip was the hardest. "This is a general. Better keep on course." Then I learned the course by heart, the towns on the way like stepping stones to Washington. As the generals rode in the aft cockpit, I could see them in my mirror but couldn't hear them, except through the earphones, which they never used. Sometimes I'd see them sunbathing back there—au naturel.

On another administration flight, with a group of Sunday school children, in a twin-engine plane, the weather suddenly closed in. This had been a special sightseeing outing as a reward for perfect attendance. We were in thick black cloud. Rain lashed the plane. Where the children had been talking excitedly, now there was silence. The teacher looked frantic.

"We'll go back, I think," I said.

Turning slowly in zero visibility, we headed in the direction of the field. One small boy was first to see it.

"There's the field," he yelled.

As we landed, I could see that the teacher was very relieved. (And perhaps that small boy is now an airline pilot.)

There were many flights where I picked up airplanes that had been left at airports for various reasons. Either it was their destination, or the plane was leaking oil, had a rough engine, and so on. I remember one A-24 dive-bomber that was said to be "leaking oil." As I flew it back to Wright Field, drops of oil dappled the windshield. The oil pressure was falling, the oil temperature rising. I slowed the engine as much as possible and limped into Wright Field as much of a wreck as the plane.

One day Sims said (again with his searching-for-birds look), "Tomorrow you get a little check ride for fighters." Pause. "With Major Lundquist. He doesn't approve of lady pilots, by the way."

"I thought Major Ritchie might have . . ."

"No. He was just being sort of a friend. He knew Lundquist was doing the test. Maybe it'll be tomorrow."

It did help to have had that preliminary flight with Ritchie.

The next morning, the AT-6 stood on the flight line. Major Lundquist was ready. We walked out to the airplane and climbed in. (The word "climb" is right. To get into an airplane from the ground, one must climb up on the wing, or steps, to enter.)

We took off and flew to the designated test area north of the field. Major Lundquist told me quietly but precisely what he wanted.

"Trim the airplane for level flight at 10,000 feet, climbing at 400 feet per minute. Do a few stalls, some lazy eights, and a two-turn spin."

I followed directions to the best of my ability, being careful to check the area for other airplanes, and finally rolled into the spin.

Suddenly the power was cut off and I heard, "Forced landing."

I recovered from the spin and headed for a large field, at this point laughing to myself, I've been here before! When he asked me where I would land, I pointed to the field.

"Okay. Do a slow roll to the right and take us back."

He said nothing after we landed and I parked the plane, but later Sims said he heard him tell Major Petrie (disappointedly?), "She actually did okay."

At last my name appeared on the test sheet. I was to test a "tail warning device," but not by myself. A very trusting (though possibly scared) FFT pilot was to fly his fighter in slow flight while I, in a single-engine dive-bomber, zoomed in behind him from all angles. The warning device was supposed to flash on when my plane was near his tail. This device from the Electronics Lab is still being improved today. But think how important it could be to a fighter or bomber in combat.

At first I was told I was not coming in close enough. So I edged in closer, right into his rough slipstream, waiting frighteningly long to turn sharply out or down, then circling back for another run. I could not be careless.

Another simpler test involved finding the radio station entirely by radio signals. I was told it was a test of early LORAN-A, soon to be a basic navigation aid. But later I found it had been in preparation for homing in on some anchored ships (native fishing boats) which would be detonated to explode over a certain tunnel between Japan's two southern islands during the war.

One day, Major Petrie handed me the technical orders (data) on the P-47 fighter.

"Read these. There might be a little test on them, so memorize the critical parts. When I locate a P-47 not in use, you can try it out. Okay?"

He did know that it would be okay. He and the others knew perfectly well how keen I was to ride aloft in a fighter plane, and had encouraged me all the way along (albeit not without a good bit of teasing).

"You're landing way down the runway. Never be able to get away with that in a fighter."

And so on. So I was ready long before the P-47 was found.

What magic did I think I would find in the driver's seat of a fighter? I pictured it as being an extension of myself soaring through the open sky. It would be like dancing, the wings my outstretched arms, the nose and engine my head and heart, the landing gear my legs. As the plane climbed effortlessly, we would leave the earth behind and balance on the thin air, higher and higher. It would be the next thing to flying with wings of my own, like a majestic Canada goose forging upward with deep wingbeats and steady skyward gaze. A fighter plane could slip through the air, hardly disturbing it. It was not an affair for a heavy bomber.

But I see myself then as young, full of the spirit of adventure and discovery, and eager to meet this new challenge. I didn't think I would be disappointed.

"Take it out and fly it for about 40 minutes," Petrie said. "But no aerobatics. Capt. Ken Chilstrom will point out all the gizmos for you."

Captain Chilstrom sat on the wing opposite the cockpit, tested me on where everything was, and helped me get the big radial engine in front of me started. It started with a semi-explosion, but quickly quieted to a steady hum. Chilstrom hopped off the wing to the ground. The linesman removed the chocks in front of the wheels, and I taxied out.

Visibility was nil in its tail-low position on the ground, so in order to see taxiing had to be done zig-zag. When cleared by the tower, I turned on to the runway and sped down it until the plane took to the air. I lifted the gear and set a steady climb out. We (the plane and I) were at 1,000 feet before we passed over the end of the runway. It seemed as though I had only to think "left turn," and it turned. I swung out of the traffic pattern into clear sky.

I pulled up into stalls, leaned over into steep turns, flipped from one lazy eight to another and got the easy, light feel of the airplane. Then I simply cruised along to take a look around. I banked sharply between white floating clouds, brushing the plane's tummy along their whipped-cream tops, ending in a straight-up climb and a low power dive. I was speeding along in a fighter plane at last. It was pure exhilaration.

Then it was time to return. I entered the traffic pattern and slowed to approach gliding speed. I kept a little power on, just to be sure, and found, because it was a heavy aircraft, that it stayed nicely on the runway after landing.

I taxied back to the FFT hangar and checked in with Sims at Operations.

"So how do you like the P-47?"

I enthused about the climb "nearly straight up" and the light feel of the controls.

"The P-47 isn't light. Wait till you fly a P-51 or a P-38," someone said.

"That's a light P-47, don't forget," Petrie said. "It's been stripped down and is an old unmodified model."

Much later, I learned what Petrie had meant by "unmodified" model, and why he had warned against aerobatics in it. Wright Field test pilots and others (including Perry Ritchie) had been responsible for the modification, and the subsequent redesign for more control in the tail section, thus producing a safer aircraft. At the time, I did not suspect that within a month an FFT pilot would be killed in this same P-47, and that much later I would come close to death myself in another early P-47. The accidents brought home the fact that a fighter plane, especially then, without the backup computers of today, could be unpredictable without warning. And there is possibly a difference between today's pilots encapsulated in pressurized cabins in pressurized flying suits, sanitized, as it were, from the world outside and supported by computers, and the 1940s pilots who were still one on one with their environment.

Another thing I would learn, quickly, about test flying was that I may have flown my last "ecstatic flying" trip. Test flying requires strict attention to speeds and pressures and performance. Sometimes it can be tiresome. But you are the doctor, carefully monitoring your patient.

CHAPTER 11

Daily Danger

The progress of aviation involves advancing the state of the art and success can only be determined by tests. During these tests, results determine things we can't do and things we should not do. Unfortunately, in testing ideas and devices, sometimes death results so that others may live.
　　—Col. Nathan Rosengarten, engineer, Head of Flight Research, Wright Field Air Force Base

One morning, as we straggled into the FFT office, we saw Lundquist and Borsodi in serious conversation with Major Petrie. As others joined in, they lost their usual perkiness.

"Ritchie was killed yesterday," Sims said. "He and his engineer. They were testing a B-25 with souped-up engines. Pulled up at high speed, low to the ground, and broke the wings off."

Ritchie, as pilot and engineer, had contributed important ideas and innovations, had flown the most difficult tests, and had always shown exuberance and given much encouragement to test-pilot beginners like myself. He was only 24 years old. Already he had been looking ahead toward space flight, toward voyaging to the moon. Books and reports on the subject were found in his rooms—showing an interest with others at Wright Field.

For the rest of us there was the urge to get out and fly, to spread our grief and memories throughout the sky. Even pilots of long experience and apparent complete control meet their deaths attempting to fulfill those tests. Each pilot begins to ask himself, "Why him? He was better than I." And he watches his own flying more carefully.

Sometimes, the deaths came more gently, and remained a mystery.

There was Captain Vavrina, for instance. He was working on assignments in the newly organized test-pilot school. He had just come down from one flight on how to test performance on a fighter and would go up again as soon as his plane, a P-40, was refueled and the oxygen topped off. He checked out with Sims, picked up his ticket, and went out. As he picked it up, we heard him say, "Well, this is all I need."

During that afternoon other fighters went off and were duly recorded on the flight sheet; when they returned, this too was recorded.

After several hours, I noticed Sims studying the sheet, then adding up some numbers. I had just done the same thing. Nothing was said though. Finally, Sims made a telephone call.

"It's half an hour beyond his available fuel limit. I just checked with the tower to see if he'd checked in to say he'd landed somewhere else."

I looked out at the line of aircraft. His was not there. We wouldn't say anything to anyone yet. But, of course, there was always another phone call. it would report a crashed plane. But what problem Vavrina fought with alone in the sky and couldn't solve we would probably never know.

Shortly after this, one of the younger FFT pilots, a Lieutenant J., did not appear for work. Someone saw him sitting in the cockpit of a P-51. We waited, but he did not come in.

Majors Petrie and Borsodi, with their own quiet suspicions, went out to see what was wrong. They stayed nearly an hour, talking seriously. The others went off on their scheduled flights. Sims and I remained at the operations desk.

At last Petrie and Borsodi returned. We knew we'd hear what went on if they wanted to tell us. If not . . .

"Take him off the schedule for a couple of days. We'll give him a little time," Petrie said.

He had said that he had lost his nerve for testing, and he felt like a quitter but couldn't seem to shake it. Petrie and Borsodi had simply told him, "Think about it a little more. Sit here if you like. Just take your time. We all have doubts from time to time. But if you should decide to really give it up, you'll just get a transfer and there will be nothing about this on your record."

This quiet understanding treatment was all he needed, it seemed. After a few days, he was back in the ready room, taking on his old tests. Nothing more was said.

Colonel Ritland liked to see the planes in the air, not sitting on the field. He encouraged the Test Section pilots to fly as many planes as possible. That included the offer to officers who were at least majors to take a non–test aircraft for the weekend, if they wanted to fly home to see their families.

One weekend, Major Petrie took advantage of that offer. He signed out a P-47 and, although the weather was marginal, flew home for a visit. It had been a long time since he had been able to get away, as he had had extra work ever since Colonel Estes left for England.

Usually, there was still some flying to be done at FFT on the weekends. I had an administration flight—someone left an aircraft in Toledo that had to be flown back.

When I returned, everyone was talking about a crash.

"Anyone I know?" I asked, expecting a "No."

"Petrie," they said.

"Oh, it can't be. Bad?"

"Killed. Low clouds, and he went straight in."

"No," I said. "No. What can we do?"

"There's nothing to do now. Maybe call his wife, if you know her."

When I got back to FFT, I saw that "my" P-47 was not on the line. Then I realized Petrie had been flying that P-47.

Borsodi was designated chief, Lundquist as assistant chief. They needed the joint arrangement, as each one was more interested in his own tasks than in administration.

At that time, Borsodi was working on P-39 flat-spin tests. This was admittedly a no-win test, but careful analysis might reveal the flaw in the aircraft's performance. A flat spin is just as it sounds. Instead of falling off into a nose-down normal spin, the P-39E model of the P-39 spun on a flat plane, like a saucer. It was difficult, maybe impossible, to recover.

Undaunted. Borsodi signed out the designated P-39 and left.

Again, Sims and I noticed later the blank space on the flight line, quietly counted off the hours, and computed the fuel time.

This time, the call came in before Sims called. There was a crashed plane, but the pilot had parachuted, was just landing in the caller's field.

Not long after that, Borsodi walked in.

"It wouldn't come out this time," he said. "But the funniest thing. It was spinning down so slowly and gently, I could stand on the wing and ride. I had to force myself to leave it."

Just another exciting day to the ex–Indy 500 driver!

Of course the crashed planes were always examined and brought back to Wright Field. I never had to be a member of the first inspection team at the crash site, though Sims sometimes was. After much detective work, what went wrong was usually discovered.

But what makes the pilot able to keep going out again and again on experimental test missions?

Fighter pilots, first of all, prefer doing their own flying, facing their own problems, alone. They look for challenges. They are confident they can meet the test, as long as they keep that protective assurance. To be "chicken," to fail to take the risk, is anathema. And most of these pilots had already flown and fought in combat.

Nevertheless, especially after a series of accidents, we, or at least I, couldn't help wondering a little as we taxied away from the line whether, for instance, that was really oxygen just loaded aboard, or whether an unforeseen failure would surprise us out there. For takeoff, however, there are too many things to do—set the propeller and the manifold pressure, check all the meters, call the control tower, check for other planes—to carry a worry for long.

And once you are in the air, back in what has become your natural world, as it were, you are looking ahead in the sky, skirting the silent, white clouds and watching the landmarks getting smaller below you. Your engine is humming evenly and the plane answers your pressures on the controls.

Nothing can go wrong.

CHAPTER 12

Talk

On rainy, windy, and low-ceiling days, we played chess or Hearts. The conversation became more relaxed, more personal than workday talk. And we had time to discuss the war, its prospects and ours.

We heard about the coon hunting at night. How they waited for a cold, moonlit night. The dogs were walked on a leash in the dark to coon country and then released. The men seemed to stand off and simply urge the dogs on, but didn't really follow them. They may have kept warm with Tennessee moonshine though. Hours later, with a great hullabaloo, the dogs treed a coon. Then the men and guns appeared and dispatched the coon—always a giant one, though sometimes only someone's cat. At least that is how I remember the story.

Of course there was talk of future aircraft—jets and rocket ships—and of future voyages in space and to the moon. On the subject of moon voyages, our RAF contingent, Wing Commander Summers and Group Captain Maurice, considered themselves the experts.

"Now, to get to the moon," Summers would begin, "you must break the trip down into its parts."

"It *can* be done, you know," added Maurice.

"Really?" asked Captain Fountain.

"How can you do it?" Major Johnston asked.

"Why, you only need to rocket off until you're out of the earth's gravity. Then you simply *fall* to the moon." (Pretty prescient back in 1943–44.)

"How do you get back?"

"That's another part of the story."

"And who will pay for it all?"

"Why, the United States. Britain doesn't have the money. Just the brains."

80

The RAF pair was famous for a flight the two once took in a Stearman trainer biplane. In fact, I saw it.

They often took up the Stearman to play around with aerobatics when the RAF planes on the field were not under tests. This time we noticed them on their final approach, and it was a rather sloppy approach, we thought. Although we waited for their flare-out before landing, they never made one and, in fact, simply allowed the plane to crash-land by itself.

They climbed out, brushed themselves off, and were heard to say, "I thought you had it, old boy."

"But I was sure you had it, old boy."

The bad weather brought visitors. We never knew who these visitors would be—some brought humor, some glimpses into current aircraft developments, some glimpses of the past. All were enlightening and bad-weather days were not wasted days.

Our most distinguished visitor was the original owner of the Huffman Prairie on which Wright Field now stood—Orville Wright. Still living in Dayton and still avidly interested in the phenomenal progress in development of the craft he and Wilbur had originally flown in 1903, he often dropped by to hear "the latest."

"When do you expect the jet here? Next week, maybe?" he'd ask optimistically. He was particularly interested in this next step in aviation—the step into jet propulsion.

He was always neatly dressed, coat and tie and hat, an overcoat if it was cool, always soft-spoken. But you listened to what he said. This man and his brother had accomplished powered aerial flight. Of course it was for them that the present field was named.

Everyone in the room edged closer to shake his hand, to wish him a good morning. And he often stopped by the operations desk and spoke to Sims and me.

"Last time we spoke," he said one day, "I asked what sort of a girl would want to fly experimental military aircraft. You didn't say," he laughed.

"Well, I guess just a sort who, instead of religiously practicing the piano, had to go out and see what was happening in the woods that day, or down at the brook, or high on the hill. And then one day she saw an airplane fly by."

He laughed again as he left, probably to check in at Bomber Test. We'd see him another rainy day, and he'd tell us again how he found it hard to believe the progress in only 40 years, from homemade engines and fabric wings to streamlined, supersonic metal aircraft with 1,500-horsepower engines, and now, unbelievably, jet propulsion.

Other visitors who would qualify as distinguished were the famous aircraft designers—Clarence "Kelly" Johnson of Lockheed's "Skunk Works," Larry

Bell from Bell Aircraft, "Dutch" Kindelberger and Edgar Schmued from North American Aviation. Sometimes, but not often, we had visitors from NACA like Bob Gilruth.

These visits were not just social calls. If they came in person, instead of sending representatives, it was because some problem had come up in the acceptance tests for the Air Force, or they had some new wrinkle in their designs. Not every one at Wright Field knew that Kelly Johnson's Skunk Works—the special and supersecret team within Lockheed Johnson established in 1943 for "Advanced Development Projects"—was working on a design for a new jet, to be designated the XP-80 Shooting Star. His P-38 Lightning was already a tactical and operational success. He was discussing aspects of the new design with Colonels Warburton and Ritland, and with Borsodi and Lundquist. The rest of us just hoped to get a glimpse of him. He was considered a tough, highly creative, salty character who had the quality of being an instinctive aerodynamicist who could "feel" a good design before he even lifted his slide rule. Ed Schmued, also a genius, with sharp features and black hair and brows, was more taciturn.

Larry Bell had a jet already built and being tested at Muroc—the XP-59A. It was the first aircraft in which jet propulsion would "marry" a basic fighter aircraft frame, meeting many new problems and making it the true pioneer into the jet age in the United States. And Bell's discussions were about plans to bring the jet—an evaluation model, the YP-59A—to Wright Field in 1944. Bell had other irons in the fire. There were tests on the P-39 and the P-63, and he was developing a helicopter. And he may have been looking ahead to the X-1 supersonic plane—the one that would take Chuck Yeager through the sound barrier in October 1947. I often visited Bell Aircraft as copilot for Maj. Ev Leach or Col. Marcus Cooper when they visited to inspect new developments, or to discuss flight procedures with Bell chief pilot Bob Stanley.

Dutch Kindelberger, as charismatic as creative and so successful, for both these reasons, in developing the P-51 for the British Purchasing Commission, now built the P-51s for the United States as well. Harry Truman, when he was senator, ordered them for us. He saw them flying during an inspection tour to Britain and realized that they performed better than our P-40. Finally, over 13,000 of these versatile fighters were built before the end of the war. Kindelberger was cordial to us all and usually greeted me with, "What did you say your favorite fighter was? Ah, yes, the P-51."

I knew I was not being considered an expert here. But I felt I was not ignored or considered out of place either by the visiting designers, or by Orville Wright.

We often had more "local" visitors on bad-weather days, pilots from the laboratories on the hill who flew tests on some of their gadgets. There were Captain Voyles, Lieutenant Bremhorst, and Lieutenant Holt, for instance. Sometimes one of them asked me to go to the officers' club on Saturday nights.

"I don't think you should go out with any of those pilots," one of the FFT pilots would say. The rest raised sham objections.

I had made it a policy not to date the FFT pilots I flew with. Of course, most of them were married, and the others had girlfriends anyway. But one day the wife of one of the pilots, Captain Onerem, called on the phone. After listening a moment, I heard Onerem say, "Oh, you don't need to worry. She's only interested in flying." A compliment, or not?

This may be a good time to note that a "report," now lost to history, had been circulated that alleged that the WASPs who were more "feminine" became better pilots than those with "masculine" characteristics. As I remember, the rumored report simply strove to prove that WASPs were normal, feminine, sexual women. Not very substantial, but we could always allude to it when certain "gentlemen" said, "Real women don't have the strength to fly military airplanes." There was a more scientific—and official—report that addressed menstrual periods' effects on women's flying skills. There were none, the report concluded.

At any rate, I had a memorable flight one day with one of the laboratory pilots, Captain Voyles. I don't think he knows, even now, what a close call it might have been. As he had never been in an A-25 Curtiss dive-bomber, I said I'd take him for a ride. With controls in the back seat, he could try it out on the way home. I can't remember what town we made our cross-country flight plan for, but I remember the "ride" well.

After takeoff, a cloud layer began to grow beneath us. As we had been told by the weather office that it would be clear all the way, we felt this cloud layer would quickly diminish. But it did not. I nosed down to get under it. Being a dive-bomber, it went down quickly. The clouds were thicker than we thought, and I happened to see something in the cloud.

A plane? No—a treetop! Up, up I went! And we sped back to clear air above Wright Field.

Last but not least was a very welcome rainy-day visitor—Rosie, or more formally, Major (then) Nathan Rosengarten, flight engineer and chief of Flight Research. He never said no when asked to accompany a pilot on a difficult test or in a new aircraft. He had once parachuted, along with Colonel Ritland, from a plywood RAF Mosquito bomber that was on fire. While he watched flames consuming the left wing, Colonel Ritland gave the order to jump. Rosie was wearing a borrowed parachute that was too big. When he kicked out the small 18- by 18-inch exit hatch, "instead of going out head first, as recommended," he said, "I went out feet first as the chest buckle of the parachute hit my chin and the chest strap across my eyes blocked my vision."

If he'd gone out head first he might have lost the parachute completely. He knew every test pilot, every engineer, and every test being flown, and loved to reminisce.

We had time, between visitors, to catch up on our newspaper reading and get some idea of the progress of the war we were fighting. As 1944 got under way, the Allies had retaken a string of South Pacific islands, starting with Guadalcanal and continuing with Guam, the Philippines, and North Burma. They had inflicted heavy losses on Japan in the Leyte Gulf.

In Europe, D-day, the cross-Channel attack, started at last on June 6, 1944. Seven hundred ships and 4,000 landing craft pounded the Normandy shores. With risk and sacrifice of life, the Allies won a toehold on the French coast and then the advance was slowed in the Battle of the Bulge in the Ardennes. Meanwhile, the Russians captured 100,000 Germans at Minsk, and a contingent of German officers led by Lt. Col. Klaus von Staffenberg plotted unsuccessfully to assassinate Hitler. German Gen. Erwin Rommel had committed suicide. And Roosevelt had won a fourth term as president. The idea of a United Nations organization for the security of peace was discussed at Dumbarton Oaks.

More war books were being published—John Hersey's *A Bell for Adano*, Catherine Drinker Bowen's *Yankee from Olympus*, Ernie Pyle's *Brave Men* among them, and popular songs being sung then included "Don't Fence Me In," "Sentimental Journey," and "Accentuate the Positive."

With this mixture of advance and frustration, it looked to us that the war was not yet winding down, though there seemed a larger pattern that gave hope of final victory. And we still had work to do at Wright Field. We would look back on this time as the golden age of aviation, where development was advancing at top speed, and yet planes were still flown by pilots, not by "wire" or computers.

As usual, we had not even finished one full game of Hearts, thanks to visitors, before the weather had cleared enough to fly tests. The flight sheet was brought up to date, and I picked up the aircraft status report from Captain Kuhn.

Borsodi's P-51 needed the barograph, strain gauges, and other instrumentation checked for more compressibility dive tests. Lundquist's new project was to make a long-range fighter out of a Spitfire. He was testing it with heavy wing-tip fuel tanks and a souped-up Packard-Merlin engine. When it was ready, he would fly it from Wright Field across the Atlantic, with fuel stops in Canada, Greenland, and Scotland, to England's Bascombe Down Test Base—England's Wright Field. Onerem was doing difficult pressure oxygen tests at different altitudes in a P-38. Fountain and Johnston were continuing Accelerated Service tests on P-47s.

I was to get time in the P-51. I'd had the "crouch on the wing" check-off, by Chilstrom again, a few days before. Now I had to familiarize myself with it before using it for tests. It seemed wicked to be helping to fight a war by playing around in the sky in this most maneuverable, most responsive, most trustworthy aircraft in order to simply familiarize myself with it, but it would certainly improve my test performance.

At the end of this day that had started out as a rainy one, and with my head still filled with the light of the sky around my aircraft, I returned to our apartment to find it empty. Sheets and towels were in a pile on the floor. Papers were strewn everywhere.

Then I found the note.

"Ann: I've been fired! Will get dishonorable discharge, they say. By spending the weekend with Charles in Chicago I went AWOL. So much for the WAACs. Sorry about it. Was nice rooming with you, and all the movies and meals and things. We had some good laughs. Well, keep flying. Maybe I'll come and visit later. I'll be in Chicago. [She left her address.] Jane."

I would miss her. What a pity to get a dishonorable discharge after the good years she had put in.

As I could not afford the apartment by myself, I was placed in a room in an Australian family's home, a little outside and south of Dayton. I would have to get a car. This was pretty hard in wartime, but my father came out and helped me find an old grey Dodge that seemed to run all right, at least until the snows came. Each morning, I had to chip the ice holding the wheels to the road before I could drive it.

Most every night I played cards with the family. Cribbage was a new game to me, with a sing-song scoring ritual that went, "Fifteen four, fifteen six and a pair is eight," and so on. They played and scored so fast that I don't know whether they beat me every time fairly or not. They had another boarder, a chap from MIT who worked at the powerplant lab. He took me out for dinner once, but we didn't seem to have much to say to one another.

Ann standing on the wing of the popular advanced trainer, the AT-6, during WASP training in Sweetwater, Texas. (Author photo)

In planes like this Cessna, women pilots built up their flying time, hoping to be accepted for WASP duty. (USAF Museum, Wright-Patterson Air Force Base)

WASP training at Sweetwater, Texas, was the same as the U.S. Air Corps cadet training—same aircraft, same discipline, same ground school. (WASP photo)

WASPs, with their parachutes over their shoulders, go out to their assigned aircraft. (WASP photo)

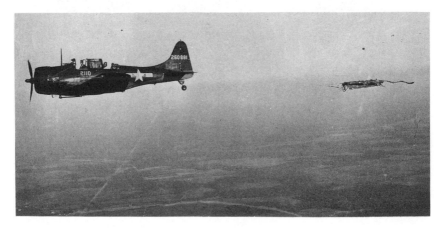

WASPs in combat-weary A-24 Douglas dive-bombers flew tow-target missions for artillery students. (WASP photo)

The B-17 Flying Fortress, in which testing began, though at first only for cold-weather clothing. (USAF Museum, Wright-Patterson Air Force Base)

The P-47, Ann's first fighter, in which she later experienced her first taste of compressibility approaching the speed of sound. (USAF Museum, Wright-Patterson Air Force Base)

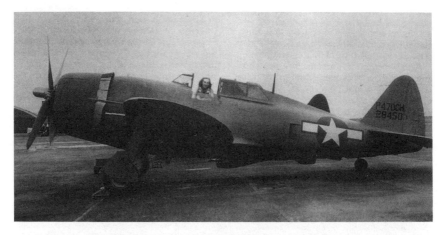

Ann in the cockpit of a P-47. ("Test Flying at Old Wright Field")

Aerial view during World War II of Wright Field, crowded with fighters, bombers, and transport aircraft. (USAF Museum, Wright-Patterson Air Force Base)

Lt. Col. Osmond Ritland *(left)*, second in command at Flight Test, and—only temporarily on crutches —Lt. Col. Harney Estes, chief of Fighter Flight Test branch. ("Test Flying at Old Wright Field")

The XP-59A during tests at Muroc in California, called Wright Field-M. (USAF Museum, Wright-Patterson Air Force Base)

Maj. Nathan "Rosie" Rosengarten *(left)*, flight research chief engineer, and Maj. Wally Lien, test pilot, discuss tests on the XP-80 Shooting Star. ("Test Flying at Old Wright Field")

Maj. Fred Borsodi, second in command at Fighter Flight Test, who was first to photograph the compressibility shock wave across the P-51 wing, and was later killed in England demonstrating the still-secret XP-80. ("Test Flying at Old Wright Field")

A historic duo, Ann and Gen. Laurence Craigie—the first woman to fly a jet and the first Air Force pilot to fly it—sit beside the National Air and Space Museum XP-59A exhibit before giving a lecture on "Fifty Years of Jet Flight." (National Air and Space Museum)

FIGHTER FLIGHT TEST

TEST	A/C	PILOT	% COMPLETE					COMPLETION DATE	PROBLEM	O.K.
			10	25	50	75	100			
Accelerated Service	P-47	JOHNSTON								
" "	P-47	LUNDQUIST								
" "	P-63	FOUNTAIN								
Power Dives	P-47	RITCHIE						6/14		✓
Flat Spins	XP-39	BORSODI							crash	
Compressibility Dives	P-51 D	BORSODI								
" " with camera	"	BORSODI								
Pressure Oxygen	P-38	ONEREM						8/10		✓
Performance	P-63	M. L. SMITH								
Tail Warning	P-51 P-51	BAUMGAATNER WALTERS								
Water Injection	P-47	JOHNSON							camera froze	
High Altitude Camera	P-38	BAUMGAATNER								✓
New A/c Evaluation	YP-59A	(SEVERAL)							not accepted	
" "	XP-77	BORSODI							not accepted	
" "	XP-62	LEACH							not accepted	
" "	XP-67	JOHNSTON							not accepted	
" "	XP-55	ESTES								
Foreign A/c Evaluation	FW-190	CHILSTROM								✓
" " "	ZERO	LIEN								✓
" " "	SPITFIRE	(SEVERAL)								✓
Pressurized Cabin Perf.	XP-47 G	BAUMGAATHER								
Long Range Test	EXP. SPITFIRE	LUNDQUIST						11/11	to England	
Off-Center Aerobatics	XP-38	(ALL)								✓
Test Pilot Course	P-40	VAVRINA							crash	
" " "	P-51	J. R. SMITH								
" " "	P-51	BREMHORST								

chart example only

Fighter Flight Test chart Ann made on orders from Colonel Estes. *(See pp. 92–93.)*

The experimental RP-38—with a cockpit replacing the supercharger in the right wing—used to test off-center flying. (USAF photo)

The XP-82, the "twin Mustang," and last propeller fighter, for which the off-center flying tests were made. ("Test Flying at Old Wright Field")

Two Fighter Flight Test pilots, Maj. Gustav Lundquist (*second from left*) and Capt. Ken Chilstrom (*far right*) raced P-80s in the Cleveland Air Races. Gus won. ("Test Flying at Old Wright Field")

Maj. Perry Ritchie, a Fighter Flight Test pilot of many dangerous tests, was the first to fly with Ann, and was later killed testing a B-25 with souped-up engines. ("Test Flying at Old Wright Field")

Orville Wright, pioneer of flight, was still on hand to usher in jet propulsion during World War II. (Walker and Wickam, *From Huffman's Prairie to the Moon*)

Maj. William Carl, liaison officer between Wright Field and the NACA (National Advisory Committee for Aeronautics), conceptual designer of the P-82 and, later, Ann's husband. (Author photo)

CHAPTER 13

Call Ann

"I could see it going across the wing!" Borsodi was saying.

"Could have been a shadow," said Rosie.

"No, it wasn't momentary. It started at the root section and I could see the wave move down the wing to the tip. I've seen it twice now."

Everyone looked skeptical.

"Let's try to photograph it then."

When a gunsight camera was installed in the P-51, the picture showed the elusive wave forming and moving down the wing. It seemed to appear near .83 MACH on the MACH meter. In compressibility, so near the speed of sound (MACH 1), the plane vibrated violently and buffeted. Control forces changed. In the P-51, this could be overcome and the plane flown out of the condition. The compressibility effects could now be calibrated with the formation and position of the wave. It was an important discovery and brought many visitors to FFT. (Ernest Mach, in about 1900, had discovered that the ratio between the speed of a body and the speed of sound varies with altitude and temperature. The MACH number became the most accurate means of measuring high speeds.)

Not every day brought important breakthroughs. For me the days were settling into a routine. I began to feel part of the operation, and, in fact, Sims had passed much of the operations work to me.

I was now called "Ann" by mechanics and generals alike. I was called to deliver messages to Borsodi or Lundquist, to receive test reports from the labs or the wind tunnel, to check on the progress of on-going tests, to check on the status of aircraft and their instrumentation, and to line up cross-country fighters (if we had one not on tests) for colonels and generals to fly.

I guess I was becoming more like bossy Jane Arbogust daily. However, I dreaded making some mistake that would take some pilot's life.

In this busy time, I was able to fit in some flying, too.

The tail warning tests continued, now using a P-51. Actually this proved to be a better test of the device, as the airplane was smaller and faster than the dive-bomber had been.

Another P-51 had a new type of gunsight to be tested. As Sims explained the test, "You fly up to this island in Lake Erie [he pointed it out on the wall chart]. There's a target on its extreme eastern tip. Turn on the gunsight and make several high-speed passes, pressing the button on the stick to shoot the guns. But first you'll have to clear the fishermen out of the area. Just buzz them and shoot off the guns. They'll get the message. They know they're not supposed to be there."

As I digested this, he added, "Wait until you think you're going to hit the target before you shoot the guns off."

Everything went as he described, even for the fishermen. I think I was the only WASP to shoot a fighter's guns in World War II! Evidently, the gunsight was a success, as it was later used. (I've often wondered what the fishermen would have thought had they known it was a woman pilot flying the P-51.)

Another device I tested was a high-altitude camera for a P-38, perhaps as an early forerunner of the cameras in the U-2 spy plane, though my altitude was only 30,000 feet. I flew a designated track at a designated speed for a designated number of times, taking pictures at designated intervals. Meanwhile, I enjoyed the view of Earth from the beautiful silver platform of the P-38, where I sat in a cockpit between the two-engine nacelles. It cried out for aerobatics and dancing in the sky, but being instrumented for speed and altitude, besides having an experimental camera, aerobatics were out.

Unfortunately, however, the camera flunked its test. It froze and took no pictures.

One day a package arrived for me from Aeromed Lab. It was the women's relief tube we had designed, now fashioned in heavy plastic. I was to test it and supply a report to Aeromed.

I did not think a fighter, which you must (or did in 1943–44) fly at all times (no autopilot), was the proper vehicle for this test. I chose instead an A-24 dive-bomber, a steady plane with fore and aft cockpits. After putting it off for a time, I finally selected a day. I climbed into the cockpit with my device and had just started taxiing out when I was called back by the linesman.

"Ann, you're supposed to take this Corporal Webb up. He needs flying time."

Before I could object (but what could I say, anyway?), Corporal Webb had himself comfortably situated in the aft cockpit.

Well, we flew around a while, while I figured out how I could decently do the test. I could see the corporal in my mirror looking out at the view. I satisfied myself that he couldn't see into my cockpit, and began unbuttoning, carefully, to do my test. I connected the device to the male relief receptacle by the long tube attached to the device, and looked back to see if the corporal was still looking outside. He was. I couldn't put it off any longer.

Our coveralls opened down the front, so I had to unbutton all the way down, steadying the plane with my left hand. I didn't want it to rock around. It might alert Corporal Webb that something was going on. So next, I had to slip the device—about 3 by 2 by 4 inches—in place, forcing it against the folds of the coveralls. I couldn't wait for a perfect positioning—what with the plane to steady and Corporal Webb to keep at bay. And so, in this precarious position, I went ahead and used the device. I didn't feel any overflow or anything, so decided it must be okay and the test done. Quickly, I brought things back to normal, coveralls, plane, tubes.

Corporal Webb was looking straight ahead now, with a rather blank look on his face. Had he seen or was he about to be airsick? I asked him on the phones if he'd like to fly the plane (he was not a pilot) and he said he would. I let him try it while I got the device back in its case. (I noticed it was dry. A good sign?)

"Try a turn, if you want to," I said. Then I took over and we returned to base. I let him climb down first, in case I had a large wet spot behind. After I checked surreptitiously that all was dry, I climbed down, too.

"Gee, thanks, Ann. I really enjoyed it. You're pretty good for a woman pilot," he said kindly.

The device was a success, I wrote in my report. It went back to Aeromed Lab, but the device never became "government issue." Today, pilots, both male and female, simply use adult diapers on long trips. This is more convenient when in a pressure suit as well.

So much for that!

Administration called me for a few cross-country flights. One was to transport a general to Indianapolis. We were in a twin-engine plane. He was in the copilot seat and he said he was in a hurry to get there.

As we flew across the Ohio countryside, I could see a squall line of thunderstorms forming to the right of us. The clouds were towering up to probably 40,000 feet. Rain slanted from their bottoms, and the air was pink and shadowy beneath them.

"You see that hole between those two thunderheads?" the general said. "Just go through there right to the airport so we won't waste any time."

I looked where he pointed. That clear spot was probably the most dangerous spot in the whole squall line. It was clear because dangerous up and down drafts and hail lived there.

"Well," I said, "I'm captain of this ship right now. And I choose to nip around the left end of this squall line as the safer route."

All he could do was grumble.

When we landed, we found that a twin-engine plane like ours had flown through that inviting hole in the squall line and had one of its wings ripped off in the turbulence there.

Another time, my passenger was a well-known professional golf champion. He and his three colleagues were appearing at a golf tournament in Louisville, Kentucky, to make money to pay for sports equipment for the enlisted men at Wright Field. This was on a Saturday.

The only problem was that he refused to fly with "any damn woman pilot."

"But there just isn't another pilot available," the general aviation operations officer told him. "Besides," he added kindly, "this is a very good pilot."

It was either not go at all or go with me, and he had to choose to go.

We settled them all into the twin-engine Beechcraft C-45, and I started off. The golf pro sat rigid, sure he was never going to see Wright Field again. We arrived in Louisville in spite of some overcast below us part of the way. When he saw the airport he relaxed, and when we landed he walked around introducing everyone to his "lady pilot." I was headed for the pilots' lounge when he called me back.

"You're invited to come along to the tournament," he called.

"That's okay, thanks. I've got a book."

"You don't want to see the golf tournament?" he said, incredulously. "Come on."

So I followed them up and down dale around the course all afternoon.

"Look at my lady pilot," he'd say to anyone around.

When finally we were back at the airplane, ready to go (it was getting dark), one of the enlisted men crew was missing. Another of the crew went to look for him. We stood around, waiting, leaning against the plane.

At last, we saw them come around the corner of the clubhouse.

"Where the hell have you been?" the pro asked.

The searched-for crew looked at us vaguely. "I ripped my trousers, sir. And then I was looking for someone to sew them up."

"What do you mean, you ripped your pants? What were you doing?"

"I caught them on a fence."

"On a fence! What fence?"

"He was just climbing over it, sir," the other crew said, helpfully.

"Let's get this straight. You were climbing over a fence. What the hell for?"

After a pause, he answered, "I just wanted to get over to the other side, sir
. . . to a trailer, to see a friend." Another pause. "She was the one who sewed
them up."

"So you were sneaking around visiting a girlfriend while we were on the
golf course. You deserved to get your pants ripped. Get in the damn plane!"

The flight home was uneventful and the whole crew slept peacefully all
the way.

Although things appeared to be rolling along rather well, and I had gained
a bit of stature in the Test Section, I began to wonder if I really had the stuff of
which test pilots are made. My forte was as a precision pilot, and that sort of
reliability is important in a test pilot. But did I have the gung-ho bravado to
throw the airplane around the sky—as Ritchie had, or Borsodi, or Lundquist?

I decided to give myself a test.

I quietly signed out an old P-47 not on tests and climbed it up to about
12,000 feet. It was a warm summer day, not a cloud in the sky. I would take the
P-47 and "wring it out" with aerobatics.

Or would I? It was like training a thoroughbred jumper who was unpredictable. I would ride him out to the training jumps, with a plan to work him
hard. But I wasn't sure until I started work whether I would really do it that
day, or should put it off to some other day when I felt braver.

Before I could change my mind, however, I started in. First a few snap rolls.
They are easy but get you in the proper frame of mind. Then a few steep lazy
eights, to climb and dive and roll in one maneuver. Then I did a slow roll,
holding the plane on its back before rolling on around. Since the P-47 nose,
with its big radial engine, is heavy, strong forward pressure is required to
hold the nose up when inverted. The next time I decided to pull the plane on
through into a dive to recover from the roll.

As we pulled through, it snap-rolled of its own accord. It continued to snap
around in the dive. The dive speeded up, and white foam, like a contrail, began
to slide across the wings. The cockpit was now full of the ages of dust gathered there; maps and papers whirled around. The control stick slammed my
knees. I eased the throttle, tried to use opposite rudder to stop the rolls, and
put the stick forward, as in a spin recovery. We were hurtling down, and the
controls were having no effect. In fact, I could hardly move them.

In our nose-down condition, I could see below me a farmer on his tractor
moving slowly back and forth across his field. I was roaring down right over him.

I tried giving the plane throttle. It was diving so fast now we were on our
back, still snap-rolling, still pulling contrails.

I decided not to jump from this plane apparently out of control. There was
the farmer to avoid and the plane was moving too fast. It must have been
screaming down. I pictured FFT at the crash scene.

After that, I simply relaxed. "Okay, God," I said. "It's up to you."

Then everything seemed to quiet down, though we still roared down. I did *not* see pictures of my past flash by. But I did feel an odd kinship with a timeless earth. Colors intensified . . .

Suddenly the controls responded. I pulled slowly, slowly back on the stick. The G-forces pulled my face down. I crouched in the seat. With a great "whoosh" the plane recovered from the dive, not more than a few hundred feet from the ground.

I carefully leveled off at 1,000 feet. I looked around at the plane and tested the controls. I looked at the Ohio countryside. Only then did I begin to shake.

Carefully, we returned to the flight line. I walked around the plane. Nothing seemed amiss. I left the plane a teller of no tales.

Surreptitious questions revealed that a P-47 required 11,000 feet to recover from a power dive, that at compressibility speeds control forces changed, and, according to Dr. Gilruth and others at NACA, early P-47s had to be modified to provide more slipstream over the tail in a dive. I had simply proved it again. But what had been there to help me? Something called luck or something more mysterious? For what was I saved?

Routine at FFT continued, and I was sometimes asked to fill in as copilot at Bomber Flight Test.

Then Lieutenant Colonel Estes returned.

CHAPTER 14

Social Flying

The atmosphere changed the minute he walked in. The door of the chief's office closed, with Lundquist, Borsodi, Johnston, and Leach inside, the rest of us outside.

He had marched in, in his long leather coat, his white scarf, flying boots, and crushed (in the Air Force manner) officer's cap. He nodded curtly to the group, stared at me, and went immediately to his desk. Then he called in the four majors and shut the door.

"That's Colonel Estes," Sims said. "He's back," he added ominously.

We attended to our operations duties quietly for the next few days. I could see Colonel Estes at his desk from where I sat. Sometimes I saw him look my way and scowl, then shake his head. I felt he was not simply being humorous, particularly when I could no longer find my name on the test sheet.

Finally, he stopped at the operations desk.

"Do you know how to make charts?"

"Charts?"

"We need a big chart on the wall to show the progress of each test. Work it out." And he walked off.

I had heard what a sterling test pilot he was, how considerate and helpful he was to new pilots. These had been men, I assumed. Female pilots evidently were beyond the pale. Yet he must have noticed women pilots, some of them American, in the Air Transport Auxiliary of the RAF while he was in England.

Charts. That would require some large cardboard, colored pencils, and so on. It also required knowledge of all FFT's tests, how far along they were, what the problems were if any, and their completion dates. Perhaps he was testing my knowledge of operations, I thought, and with Sims's help I found out things I had merely glossed over before. Until the chart was finished, there was to be no flying for me.

When it was, in all its glory, tacked up on the wall, I had done all Colonel Estes seemed to want me to do, and I was transferred, without further explanation, to Bomber Flight Test (BFT).

Fortunately, I had already met many of the Bomber Test pilots and had flown as copilot with some, including the BFT chief, Maj. Robert Ruegg. Major Ruegg was a soft-spoken, patient, ex-combat pilot who felt that it was a privilege to be part of the experimental test center at Wright Field—which indeed it was. BFT, also, had already had a female in their midst, Captain Arbogust, and had not minded it.

Life at BFT was very different from FFT. It was more convivial, more relaxed, warmer, more laughter, more talking. And this spilled over into the cockpit environment, too.

Best of all, there seemed to be a constant need for an eager copilot. And standing in as copilot on the various bomber tests, I learned from the experienced bomber test pilots—like Ruegg, Ralph Hoeing, Jack (Pappy) Williams, Russ Schleeh—how tests should be flown, as well as how to fly each aircraft. However, it was assumed you could fly the airplane. You were now finding out if the aircraft itself met the advertised specifications.

There were performance and cross-country tests on the North American twin-engine B-25 bomber (whose noisy engines were right outside the cockpit windows). And similar tests on the Martin B-26, both the short-wing and modified longer wing models. New propellers and souped-up engines were tested on the B-17 Flying Fortress bomber to get it to 43,000 feet, new landing gear on the B-24 four-engine Liberator bomber. Often, I was allowed to fly "left seat," as pilot.

To check off as first pilot of a bomber, besides general ability to fly the craft, you had to show you could take off or land with one or more engines out. Your pilot acting as instructor would surprise you as you were doing takeoffs and landings and, without a word, quietly cut the throttle on an engine or two. Part of the test was to realize an engine was out, which one, and immediately begin compensating. The plane had to be kept going straight with strong rudder pressure against the torque of the working engine. If it had been "for real," the prop of the engine out would be feathered to cut down drag. More power must be applied. The nose must not come up and cause a stall. If there is time, some of these pressures can be held with trim tabs. With two engines out on one side, more power on the two good engines, will, of course, be too much to hold with the rudder alone. On takeoff, in a climb with the nose high, the nose must be dropped in an engine failure and power added judiciously to avoid a stall. In a stall, the plane has lost flying speed and the will to fly.

Bomber Flight Test had several foreign planes to test. The British Lancaster bomber and the plywood Mosquito bomber, as well as the German twin-engine light bomber, the Ju-88. I was able to fly copilot in the Lancaster and Observer copilot in the Mosquito and the Ju-88.

The Mosquito was a small twin-engine bomber. Ours had been built in Canada, and its performance was to be compared with the RAF version from Bascombe Down, England's test base. Pilots seemed to prefer it to the Canadian one.

One morning a Lieutenant F. asked me to fly in a Mosquito with him to record test data. We taxied out and stopped at the end of the runway to go through the pre-takeoff checklist. We went through it several times, and the lieutenant still seemed uncertain, but we took off and ran through some abbreviated tests. I did not feel that the lieutenant was comfortable in the aircraft and was glad to come in and land.

Later, I discussed the flight with one of the FFT pilots, Captain Fountain, I think.

"Oh, Lieutenant F.! Don't fly with him again. Better stick to the old-timers."

I thought perhaps he was joking again, but one afternoon there seemed to be an emergency on the runway. It was a four-engine bomber, with one engine out. It was hard to see what the problem really was, but we saw it approach and then pull up and come around again. That time, however, it crashed beyond the runway, killing all aboard. The pilot had been Lieutenant F.

I was fortunate to be part of two important bomber tests. One was an early air-refueling test. It was an attempt to stretch the range of fighters protecting long-range bomber flights. The other involved heavily loaded, long-range flights in the B-29 Superfortress, to test its capability to carry a new bomb weighing about 9,000 pounds and measuring about 10 feet by 28 inches. Of course we jumped to the conclusion it was for an atom bomb, but we were laughed at. "It's just a heavy bomb," we were told. "No one has an atom bomb yet."

For the air-refueling, I was copilot to Maj. Russ Schleeh, one of BFT's best and most experienced pilots, in the B-24 that acted as tanker. Major Borsodi flew a P-38 Lightning, acting as the plane requiring fuel. While we held the four-engine B-24 in slow flight at about 10,000 feet, Borsodi cut one engine on the P-38 so that he could come close under the B-24 to attach the makeshift nozzle. We had the bomb-bay doors open so that we could look down to see whether he could attach. It was like watching a fish take bait. After several runs, Borsodi started for home. He could not restart his engine, however. We followed him back in case, with only one engine, he was not able to keep the P-38 from cartwheeling into the dead engine. He landed it, however, without incident.

On the B-29 long-range tests, we carried our heavy dummy load all over the American sky for many hours. Our load had to equal 8,900 pounds and fill an area 10 feet by 28 inches. Now we know these were indeed the measurements needed for the "Little Boy" atom bomb, but we were not supposed to even think it then. Our long-range requirements must have been for a very long flight through the Pacific islands, we thought, perhaps all the way to Tokyo.

Maj. Fred Bretcher was the pilot. I, as one of the alternating copilots, and the rest of the crew were able to watch the light over the land turn pink and then fade into darkness from 30,000 feet. We were then alone with the stars, until dawn crept over the land from the east. The off-watch crew found places to curl up and sleep in the darkened, droning plane. There was a certain boredom as the hours stretched out that would possibly not be present if we were the B-29 chosen to actually deliver the "heavy" bomb.

As part of this project, we made flights from Wright Field to Wendover Field in Utah, where the 509th B-29 Bomb Squadron and Colonels Paul Tibbets and Sweeney awaited parts and repairs for problems on their B-29s resulting from engine overheating. They had been selected to deliver the "heavy" bomb. As the atom-bomb factor was continually denied, we at Wright Field were not subjected to any special secrecy provisions. Our job was to simply make the basic preparatory flight tests and to keep Colonel Tibbets's *Enola Gay* in flying condition with the parts and advice he needed from Wright Field.

Major Bretcher gave me some "left-seat" time in the B-29, with the usual engine-out procedures, though, unfortunately, with not enough time for complete check-off. What I remember most about the B-29 was the fact that the glass nose of the plane distorted the view ahead of the runway. The pilot actually aimed to the side of the runway. Otherwise, except for engine overheating, it was easy to fly.

This casual checking-off in aircraft was usual between Flight Test pilots, and I naturally fell into the process—and felt honored to be included. Flight Test pilots felt a fellow accepted Flight Test pilot was simply qualified to fly airplanes.

Some of the most memorable bomber flights were the evening rides as copilot for Col. James Gillespie in a B-17 (usually the same one). Colonel Gillespie dreaded being forced to accept a generalship and a desk job and not being able to fly anymore. We would go up and fly around, sometimes just sightseeing, sometimes going through various maneuvers. Often, he would turn it over to me to fly while he looked around at the sky and smiled to himself.

Unlike those at FFT, the BFT pilots' wives invited me to join them for family picnics and parties. We went swimming. We went to amusement parks. And sometimes, I went to their Saturday night drinking parties. In fact, if I did not go, I was called a party-pooper. The parties, at someone's house—I can't remember whose—involved drinking, singing, and sitting around. And there was a room where some couples, one at a time, would disappear for a while. It seemed to me to be an evening of forced fun, but during wartime, in a place far from home, where you were doing work that could endanger your life, even forced fun can ease some of the stress.

Every few months there were banquets celebrating achievements and anniversaries. The BFT families included me, and as neither Orville Wright nor I had spouses, we were usually seated together—one famous man and one odd-ball WASP! So many stopped to speak to Orville that there was little time left for conversation. What there was centered on the expected YP-59A.

"You must fly it and tell me how it flies," he would say.

But every one of us fortunate enough to chat with him knew it was a rare chance to act momentarily as a link between the very beginnings of aviation and the next phase of jet and rocket flight.

I appreciated the cordiality of the BFT wives in including me in the after-hours life at Wright Field, but I never exactly felt at home there. I did not have their problems—housework, children, and school. Rather, I was, in fact, in the position of their husbands, doing the work they were doing. There was always a sort of barrier where they kindly entertained a lone "girl" who was nearly their age but had nothing in common with them but their husbands' work.

Wartime should have made a difference, and if I had not been the lone WASP there it would have, perhaps, too. Of course, now, 50 years and many changes in lifestyles later, this condition would be the norm rather than atypical.

It had been pleasant at BFT to fly "in company" rather than as a lone pilot, and I had been able to fly important bomber tests and check off in the bombers as well, but when I was recalled to FFT it was good to know that I had not been sent to BFT by Colonel Estes as a demotion, and that I was chosen to return when a pilot was needed. I felt a real part of FFT and was glad for a chance to show loyalty to it.

CHAPTER 15

Return

Although there were no welcome posters, it was enough that they wanted (even needed) to have me back. Outside on the flight line were many new airplanes from the aircraft companies to test. And there were several foreign fighters: the British Spitfire, the German Me-109 and FW-190, and the Japanese Zero. And finally, there was our first jet-powered plane, the XP-59A.

Some of the new planes looked pretty odd. They were essentially attempts to solve problems.

The XP-77, from Bell Aircraft, was a tiny, plywood craft painted a sickly green. It was designed to outmaneuver the lightweight, unarmored Zero. It showed its descendancy from the P-39 and P-63, but the pilots that flew it characterized it—at best—as a toy. Bell had gone too far to make it light.

Several of the new planes were designed strictly for high speed. The Mc-Donnell XP-67, for example, tried for smoother streamlining, with huge fillets between fuselage and wings to ease the air over the connecting corners, but it did not add appreciable speed. The XP-55, on the other hand, from Curtiss, was a canard, with the tail in front of the wing, and was dubbed by skeptical pilots as the "ass-ender," but it did not climb as advertised.

In other attempts for high speed, there was the XP-72, so full of turbo jet piping it was a plumber's dream, but not a pilot's, and the General Motors XP-75, which had two counter-rotating props.

Then there was the RP-47E (R = restricted) with the first fighter pressurized cockpit. This was supposed to end run the pressurized oxygen problem and allow the fighter pilot to reach altitudes above 45,000 feet.

Finally, there was the early model of our first jet-powered aircraft, the Bell YP-59A fighter. As it was still "secret," it had to be parked with a false propeller attached to hide the fact that it was a jet plane.

All these planes would be compared to the foreign planes in performance, speed, maneuverability, and stability.

Sims informed me that I was assigned the RP-47E with the pressurized cockpit to do performance and flight characteristics testing at altitude. The plane was instrumented, including the barograph, and I was, in the regular test-pilot fashion then being taught in the Wright Field Test Pilot course, equipped with a data pad strapped to my knee. I would, in a sequence of tests, find out whether the added pressurized cabin configuration affected the speed, rate of climb, and stall characteristics of the airplane at different altitudes. The viability of the pressurization itself was not part of the test schedule. Though that was assumed, I was to use oxygen.

The first test of the RP-47E was at 25,000 feet. It was evident in the climb to altitude that it would require higher power settings than those prescribed to approach the proper rate of climb. Even at level flight it required greater power settings. It stalled sooner and was, in general, rather a dog. Nevertheless, I had to record exact differences. I also had to watch the fuel gauges carefully, as the extra power requirements used more fuel. I didn't need another dead-stick landing.

Although it was back to the drawing board for the aircraft companies, as none of these new planes answered in full the needs of the Air Force for a long-range fighter or for more speed and maneuverability, they did contribute new engineering ideas for further development.

We FFT pilots were able to fly some of the foreign planes, but the actual definitive tests on them were done by Estes, Borsodi, Chilstrom, Schleeh, and Lundquist. Lundquist's determination was that the three best fighters in World War II were the U.S. P-51, the British Spitfire, and the German FW-190, with the P-51 best in total performance and stability.

The jet stood a little apart on the flight-line apron, an armed guard beside it. The longer it sat there, the more attractive it looked. Who would be allowed to fly it? Colonel Ritland at last announced, "Certain FFT pilots, and that includes the WASP, who will be the first woman to fly a jet aircraft."

Other than Colonel Estes, Borsodi, and Lundquist, and perhaps Chilstrom, we at FFT really knew little about the low, streamlined, twin-engine fighter, in its dark camouflage colors, sitting quietly on the taxiway in front of our hangar. Its preliminary tests had all been made at Muroc Dry Lake in California ("Wright Field West"), both for the sake of secrecy and because of its early need for a long takeoff run. Even now it had its Air Force Guard and fake four-bladed propeller.

We had heard, of course, that it was coming, and that its turbo jet engines were of British design and General Electric–built, and that its fuselage was a combined Wright Field–Bell Aircraft design, built by Bell. Most important, though, it stood for the fact that jet propulsion worked!

What was completely secret then—the difficult evolution of this first jet— was explained after the wraps were off, with detailed accounts in, for example, GE's own record, *Flame Powered*, by David Carpenter of GE, in Grover Heiman's *Jet Pioneers*, and from my husband, who was at NACA in those years.

In the early 1940s, several nations—Italy, Germany, Britain, and Japan— were doing preliminary work on turbo jet and rocket propulsion for aircraft. In Germany, Dr. Hans von Ohain had developed a turbojet engine and secretly tested it in a He-178 on August 27, 1939. Then, with Germany's attack on Poland that year, the Reich supported further development. Both Italy and Japan had made short trial flights with early jets in the 1940s. In Britain, Frank Whittle, working without government support or interest, had patented a jet engine in the 1930s. Under a contract with the British Power Jets firm, the little turbo jet engine powered a flight by a Gloster aircraft (the "Squirt") on May 15, 1941.

In the United States, rumors of German work on jets spurred research here. Maj. Don Keirn at Wright Field had read about the Whittle patent and the Gloster flight and was sent to England by General Arnold to evaluate Whittle's work. The result was Arnold's decision to have GE, with its wide experience in turbo superchargers, further develop the Whittle engine here, and for Bell, with Wright Field assistance, to build a compatible airframe—all in a state of extreme secrecy and speed.

Whittle's W1X engine was flown in a B-24 from Prestwick, Scotland, on October 2, 1941. Only one year later two GE 1A engines were finished and running, the fuselage nearly ready.

Bell, chosen by Arnold and GE to build the P-59A because of his enthusiasm and attention to detail, incorporated new features in the airframe. Not only did the jet engine require special designing for intakes, cooling, and exhaust, but the two engines had to be close to one another to reduce drag and to avoid difficulties in case of sudden single-engine flight. As this created boundary-layer turbulence along the fuselage, a boundary-layer bleed system was designed. And, as the plane was designed then for high-altitude performance, its wings were long and of low-drag laminar flow design.

The plane weighed 9,000 pounds, had a wing span of 49 feet, and a total length of 38 feet. The tail section "curved high to ensure clearing the jet wake." Among its new "jet" instruments—a tachometer reading up to 18,000 rpm, tailpipe temperature gauges, bearing temperature gauges—was a "vibrator." Due to the smoothness of the jet engines, the vibrator had to shake the instrument needles.

On September 12, 1942, the completed XP-59A was prepared for shipment to Muroc for its test flights. At midnight, two crates, one for the fuselage and the other for the two wings, were slowly set down by crane on the railroad flatcars. To protect the bearings from the bumps and starts of the train, a gas-powered air compressor would keep the engines turning slowly. The two flatcars and a passenger car for the Air Force, GE, and Bell crews were attached to the "Red Ball" California-bound fast freight.

The trip proved to be an adventure. First, during the night, a U.S. Marines flatcar marked "HIGH EXPLOSIVES" was coupled in ahead of them. The crew had to persuade the railroad to move the explosives car to the end of the train (the railroad replaced it with a carload of sheep). While that was being done, the crew went for a hot meal in a nearby restaurant. On their return, they couldn't find their flatcars. A policemen finally located them. Then dirty gas in the compressor kept the crew busy adjusting it. Meanwhile, as they were shuttled about and parked on sidings, Wright Field and Bell did not know exactly where their jet was. It finally arrived at Muroc after a six-day trip.

Bob Stanley, Bell chief test pilot, made the first test flight on October 2, 1942. Col. Laurence Craigie was the first Air Force pilot. When now–Lieutenant Colonel Keirn finally got to fly it, the fuel pump quit, making him the first to make a dead-stick landing in it. Major Wally Lien from Wright Field FFT did the Air Force testing of the XP-59A at Muroc.

The goal in the XP-59A had been to produce a production jet fighter right away (equipped with three .50-caliber machine guns and two 37mm cannon), not just a single test-prototype. There were three XP-59As. Tests on them were mainly on engine problems. Performance testing (this time with Bell pilot Jack Woolams) was done on the YP-59A version with squared-off wingtips and vertical stabilizer and the improved I-16 engine instead of the original GE-1A. Thirteen were built, two going to NACA for full-scale wind-tunnel spin tests, one to Wright Field, and the rest for miscellaneous tests.

The Bell Muroc testing program was completed in February 1944. Would our group evaluation on October 14, 1944, agree with the Muroc tests?

A group gathered early at the YP-59A that warm, sunny October morning at Wright Field. The jet was to be started up, and the first group—Flight Test Division colonels and majors—would fly it. Suddenly the morning quiet was blasted with the first jet engine start-up. Black smoke and red flame exploded from one engine tailpipe, then the other. Everyone on the field came to attention. Necks craned to see what was happening. The YP-59A's secret was blown. Everyone now knew this was the jet plane.

We watched it slowly taxi out to the runway. No trouble seeing or hearing its screaming engines. After a moment's hesitation at the end of the runway, it turned and roared ahead for takeoff, taking most of the runway to get off into a shallow climb-out. We watched it disappear, trailing a jet stream but no smoke or flame. There would be jet fuel for only 30-minute flights—enough for only an abbreviated examination, but enough to get the feel of jet-propelled flight. We awaited our turns anxiously, hoping the brass were taking good care of the jet.

Right after lunch, it was my turn. Major Lien met me at the plane, and I climbed in. Tall, slim, and reserved, he was an outstanding test pilot and aeronautical engineer. He crouched on the wing, looking into the cockpit.

"The first thing you must know," Lien said, "is that you'll have to land first time around. The slower acceleration of power in the jet will not get you off and around again."

Then he pointed out the tailpipe and bearing temperature gauges, and their red-lined positions. He explained, briefly, how the jet works—sucking in air, turbos jetting it out behind, pushing you ahead.

"Compare it generally with other fighters. Is it as fast, as stable, as maneuverable? And enjoy yourself," he said, as he jumped off the wing.

I was alone with the jet. Weighed down with responsibility. I advanced the power and the engines whined, black smoke trailing. Visibility with the tricycle gear was good, and taxiing could be controlled just with the rudder. Cleared for takeoff, I pushed the engines to a high scream and started down the runway. As advertised, it took a while to get airborne. Settled into the climb, suddenly the engine noise stopped. Had the engines quit already?

No, we (the plane and I) were still climbing. Then I realized the jet noise was now behind me. I looked out at the elliptical wings and the narrow nose ahead of me. As we slid along silently, it was strange to realize I was the only jet up there, perhaps the only jet over the United States that day.

Trimmed out at about 8,000 feet, at 16,000 rpm the I-16 engine could produce 1,600 pounds of thrust and an airspeed less than 400 MPH, about 390. I noticed I had to keep correcting our course slightly—it did not quite track, which showed a lack of stability that would be troublesome as a gun platform in combat. Its turning radius, in steep turns, was very good. Stalls with its long wings were gradual. In a spiral it was stable in the turn and did not "wind up" dangerously. We had been told that it was still difficult to recover from a spin and not to try them. Too soon, it was time to return.

The landing was uneventful. The jet landed squarely on its tricycle gear. Again, amid screaming engines and black smoke (like the jets today) we taxied back, safe and sound. I admit, I did wonder idly whether a local reporter might be there to check on the first woman to fly a jet, but, of course, the project was still very much a secret, and others from FFT had flown it that day as well, the men, that is. Actually the "first" was to remain unchallenged for ten years.

When I checked in with Sims, he said, "Add your comments to the evaluation report. Then there's a general who needs to be taken to Detroit this afternoon."

So it was just another day at FFT! And no time to discuss our evaluations.

Sims then told me that Colonel Estes had been watching from the control tower—biting his nails perhaps—but also it could have been that in case of engine failure he'd be ready with advice. (The early XP-59As had to have their engines taken out and overhauled between flights.)

The final Air Force evaluation of the X and Y P-59As was issued June 28, 1945. It concluded that "even though a combat airplane did not result from the development of the X and Y P-59A airplanes, it is considered that the development was worthwhile since it proved that the principle of jet propulsion for aircraft was sound and practical."

Fifty P-59As were built for demonstration.

Building on the P-59A experience, the next step in jet propulsion was already taking form in the "Skunk Works" of Lockheed—the XP-80. But before it was ready, Allied pilots were to see a German fighter without propellers, the German Me-262 jet, in the skies over France in the final days of the war in Europe. The Germans had even tried rocket power in their Me-163, though they did not develop it further.

But the step had been made into the jet age.

CHAPTER 16

Winding Down

In October, there was news from Washington for all WASPs. Without exception, the WASPs would be disbanded the end of December 1944.

Although it was true that fewer pilots were being requested for European duty, the war seemed far from finished there and certainly continued to rage, with high losses on both sides, in Asia. The German thrust in the Battle of the Bulge still awaited General Patton's brilliant rout. Germany's demise had not yet been achieved.

However, the public and small business had quietly begun to urge the War Production Board to allow a start in the production of civilian goods, though Roosevelt vetoed it. But, more important to WASPs, the instructors in the government Civilian Pilot Training Program who had gratefully accepted their exemption from Air Force cadet training and combat now suddenly decided they would like to take over the WASP flying jobs in this country. Although they did not have comparable training, and although the WASPs had signed on knowing and accepting all risks involved, nevertheless, the CPTP pilots had gathered support and sympathy in Congress.

Foreseeing loss of status through misinterpretations of the WASPs' true part throughout the war effort, Jackie Cochran had been working steadily for militarization in the Air Force for the WASP. General Arnold, though as eager as Cochran for gaining status for the WASP, had not been successful in persuading Congress to pass this enactment. Instead, Cochran's training program was shut down, and active WASPs were offered militarization in the WAAC, where Cochran knew all connection with their true place in the Air Force would be lost. Cochran, at this time, was in poor health, and now faced disappointment in her efforts to assure a place in aviation history for the WASP contribution in World War II.

So, with the WASP highly expert and often dangerous military flying still secret, in December 1944 we would turn in our equipment—uniforms, parachutes, jackets, oxygen masks, coats, boots, gloves—while we felt there was still flying work to be done. We would suddenly be civilians, without military benefits. Not even the G.I. Bill applied to us. The civilian instructors, however, were taken into the Air Force, individually, following the usual Ferry Command practice.

Although it took a while to adjust to the new outlook—or, rather, lack thereof —there were still, in the short time left, some interesting flights for me at Wright Field, though there would be no chance of further jet flights, especially in the XP-80. Each flight was made with a special realization of having been part of the immense war effort worldwide, and of having this chance to fly these military airplanes in this professional context. Each flight was a sort of goodbye.

I was given a P-47 to fly down to Orlando, Florida, where I would be picked up by a B-17 that was scheduled to fly from Orlando to Wright Field. The P-47, being a test aircraft, did not have full cross-country navigational equipment. There was only a small radio on the floor of the cockpit to pick up the radio range signals (no OMNI, LORAN, or GPS then); running on battery power only, it could not be used for long periods. When clouds gathered over the mountains of Tennessee, I had to lean down to the floor, tune the radio to the proper range station without being able to see the numbers on the radio, and also keep the plane in level flight.

It all worked out, with a fairly short trip through the fascinating grey-cloud country, where folds of overlapping clouds are suddenly pierced by white cloud towers and long vistas stretch away beyond. I landed in Orlando just before dark.

Back at Wright Field, a report came in that a P-47 had crashed in the mountains. Later, my arrival report reassured them that my plane had reached its proper destination. I was just a rider on the B-17 return flight. I rode in the nose and watched animals in the fields below, farmers at work, the rivers and valleys and towns of the Midwest, all at minimum altitude.

From time to time combat aces were assigned to Wright Field. Capt. Don Gentile was one, and, like most aces, he did not feel constrained by either the delicate instrumentation in test aircraft or the landing rules of the airport. (Other test pilots did not welcome being jumped by recent aces for a little sport while they themselves were doing precision tests either.)

One day, Gentile, in a test aircraft, did a bit of serious "buzzing" of his girlfriend's house in Columbus. He was promptly grounded and I, the WASP, was sent to both embarrass him and transport him back to Wright Field. He accepted this, nevertheless, with good grace and humor.

Colonel Ritland encouraged me to check off in all the planes I could before the axe fell.

"You have never been aggressive about flying planes we haven't given you to fly," he said. "But perhaps that's why you got to fly so many."

"Well," I said, "I simply appreciate being part of this important place, flying with the cream of the Air Force."

I rushed to fly, then, a C-47, the Douglas DC-3, the elder statesman among transport planes, and a favorite of all pilots who have flown it. And I gathered check-offs in other civilian planes sitting around in General Aviation: Stinson Reliant, Staggerwing Beechcraft, the PT-17 Stearman trainer, Travelair, and especially the Canadian Workhorse, the Nordyne Norseman.

Then I thought about the helicopter. I'd never get another chance.

"Planes in the CARGO hangar are not for the likes of fighter pilots," the FFT pilots told me. And like the fighter pilots, I did not fly one. A lamentable mistake. I might have finally flown a flying ambulance, then, too.

Finally, there was just one serious FFT test left.

In the search for a long-range, high-speed fighter, an Air Force major and aeronautical engineer assigned as liaison officer between NACA and Wright Field came up with the idea of putting two P-51s together. There would be two fuselages separated by a wing section, with two cockpits, one in each fuselage. But would the pilot flying off center feel comfortable and properly in control in this position?

To find out, Wright Field replaced the large supercharger in one nacelle of a P-38 with a small "cockpit." We rode in the cockpit while a colleague "wrang us out." Did we feel disturbingly off-center? All who took part agreed that there was no problem. The conceptual design for a twin Mustang then became the fastest prop-driven fighter, the XP-82, with, in addition, the longest range. Eight hundred were built to serve in the latter part of World War II and the Korean War.

The major came up to Wright Field from time to time during this test program. Between test flights, he passed the time in the FFT office, usually sitting directly across from the operations desk.

He had all sorts of interesting things to say, funny stories to tell, and seemed to me a courteous and thoughtful gentleman.

Bill Carl was his name. He had grown up in a large family of cousins and uncles and aunts on Long Island, had graduated from Princeton as an engineer and had been drafted on the first draw. From a stint with General Patton, he transferred to the Air Force. After training at Chanute Field, he was transferred to New Hampshire (where he kept A-20s that were equipped for desert warfare flying in the snow and ice of New Hampshire by injecting ether into the engines with a berry-spraying outfit, not without a fire or two).

Then he went to Trinidad. As a major he finally was sent to NACA at Langley Field, Hampton, Virginia, as liaison officer with Wright Field.

He had been a sailor since the age of 8, when a man who owed his father money gave him a small sailboat as payment. He planned someday to cruise the whole coast of the United States. In the meantime, he had designed a rigid airfoil sail that he was testing out with Bob Gilruth on Back River at Langley Field.

Even as a small lad he went cruising in his sailboats. Once he and a friend started off to sail down Long Island's Great South Bay. The first night it rained hard, so they headed for a quiet dock, tied up, rigged a tarpaulin over the boom, and lit up their sterno stove to cook supper.

Suddenly, loud footsteps approached on the dock. A man tore back the tarpaulin.

"Boys, what are you doing here? This is a girls' orphanage! Just untie your boat, and tie up somewhere else."

They sailed off in the rain and anchored.

Another time, after spending an afternoon on Coney Island's famous rollercoaster, he and a cousin decided to build one. There was some oak flooring for an uncle's new house lying around, so they nailed it up with big nails to take a wagon from atop the chicken coop down into the pigpen, which could be filled with water. The first calamity was one pig, who died of fright. The second was that Bill's father was so enraged at this wanton use of the expensive oak flooring that he grabbed the whole structure and shook it, tore his clothes, and fell into the water.

Who could resist an inventive background like this? Not I.

After this rather romantic way of meeting, and after just three dates, we fell in love and were married five months after the WASP disbandment, and four days after V-E Day, on May 12, 1945.

CHAPTER 17

Last Flights

Just as there had been no welcome posters when I returned to FFT, there were no formal goodbyes. This was the tradition. The life of FFT continued. There was a war on and, just as the deaths had not been talked about, any feeling of loss was internalized, to be looked at later. The words "goodbye" were anathema, like the superstition that the words "good luck" to an actor on opening night are bad luck.

Both Lundquist and Borsodi left for flights to England, without goodbyes.

Lundquist left in his fuel-rich Spitfire to prove that a Spitfire could be a long-range fighter. There was no fanfare. He had test-flown it with its extra internal and exterior wing tanks, figured out his route and fuel stops, and taken off.

Borsodi was flown to England in a bomber. We had heard only secondhand that he was gone. His flight in England was to be a secret demonstration of the still-experimental XP-80, and it was tucked away, dismantled, in the bomber.

I did not leave the Flight Test Division completely right away. I moved over to the public relations department, where I (having been a writer for the *New York Times*) hoped to do stories on these test-pilot heroes who, after years in combat, now willingly flew dangerous tests to eliminate hazards in the planes future Air Force pilots would fly. And recently, two more of the test-pilot heroes, Zed Fountain and M. L. Smith, had crashed in experimental planes. Yet I noticed that most of my stories were filed away for after the war. And I found that not only was Wright Field more interested in suppressing publicity than advertising itself then, but of course it was not at all interested in publicizing what was happening to the country's combat pilots and what dangers awaited them as test pilots. My hope of bringing their stories to public attention was dashed. I did not stay long.

My last flight from Wright Field was in early February 1945. It was not strictly authorized. It was an arrangement of convenience. Major Leach needed a copilot for his B-24 flight to Mitchell Field, New York, and I lived in New York. Though listed officially as a passenger, I would be the copilot. I climbed aboard in my civilian clothes and high heels and sat in the copilot seat, and on the flight did the copilot tasks.

Just before we left, Rosie handed us a piece of folded paper.

"Read it after you get airborne," he said.

When we reached our altitude and leveled off, I opened the note and read it aloud. "This morning Major Fred Borsodi was killed when his XP-80 exploded over England."

Neither of us spoke after hearing this shattering news. Rosie knew how deeply this would affect us and knew we could work it out best in flight.

About an hour out, Leach leaned over and said, "I'm feeling kind of rocky today—the flu, I guess. I think I'll go back and stretch out for a while. Report in to Air Traffic Control at Pittsburgh if I'm not back."

Although Leach had the plane trimmed out for level flight at about 8,000 feet, the B-24 is, so to speak, a wallower. Small corrections are needed to keep it on track. The weather was forecast to be clear though hazy most of the way.

I was alone in the cockpit, looking out at the farmland country as it passed below. The sky was bright, reflecting the haze, with a few cirrus mare's tails high above.

This would certainly be the last time I would fly a B-24, or any bomber probably. But how extraordinary that I should be flying one at all. Without Jackie Cochran's program, bringing so many of us (about 1,000 altogether) into the war effort, we would not have had this great chance to fly military planes.

Had we been a help? What, essentially, we did, and I did, was to be extra hands. We spread out the burden of necessary flying for carrying on a war. We were other fingers in the dike.

I felt we had been pioneers as military pilots flying military aircraft. None had gone before us. In answering the need for pilots in wartime, we had changed women's status in flying forever. We had proved women could be professional pilots. Many, after our lead, would follow us. Looking ahead, I could see their achievements would be in different kinds of flying, in planes run by computers, heavier and faster, in novel helicopters and support craft. And, finally, women pilots would captain jets for the airlines and would even fly in space. Although WASPs, at that time, could not aspire to fly in combat, later U.S. women may even fly there, as the Russian women have.

Certainly, aviation provides a fulfilling career for women. And that they can fly professionally was proved in World War II.

Over Pittsburgh, I checked in: "Air Force B-24 en route Mitchell at 8000. Estimate Newark sixteen twenty three."

We would start our descent to Mitchell after crossing the busy traffic area over LaGuardia and (then) Idlewild.

As we bored ahead on our course, engines droning, the cockpit empty, I looked ahead for myself. Would I continue flying? I was superstitious, too. Had I used up my flying luck? There had been times when I had stretched it. To fly is a privilege. It gives a special view of life—objective, quiet, extended. But as exhilarating and challenging as flying is, was it, for me, enough? There was medicine, still. I had not flown a flying ambulance in the war, as I had hoped, though the flying I did I could not have imagined beforehand. The friends I had met would always be important, and one was to be my husband soon.

I thought back to the question Orville Wright had asked as we stood—it seemed long ago—in front of the FFT hangar and watched Fred Borsodi taxi in his P-51.

"What kind of a girl are you to want to fly an experimental jet?"

Whatever "kind of girl" I had been then had changed, I thought. Instead of a young, somewhat brash, fledgling flyer, eager to challenge the sky in any Air Force fighter or bomber, I was, in some ways, more serious and, in other ways, more confident. The strict regimen of test flying had given me an understanding of the laws of physics that produced flight and, at the same time, restricted it. My carefree joy of flying was tempered now by a new focus on strict performance of the aircraft. Had I performed adequately at FFT and BFT to be able to consider myself a member of that test-pilot band?

There was something else—something bigger than my own accomplishments. It had to do with being a part, a small part, with my colleagues at Wright Field, in winning the war against the evil forces of Nazism.

And with all of this, I had come to know the very first man in aviation, Orville Wright. I had experienced the effects of the sound barrier—the effects of compressibility—and had, also, been a pioneer into the jet age.

Yet, too, I had a more profound appreciation of the capricious nature of mortality. I looked finally, then, at the deaths we had had at FFT. There were new ones, and later others would be added. Ritchie . . . Petrie . . . Vavrina . . . Fountain . . . Smith . . . and now, Borsodi. Pilots have come to believe that a God, an angel, a mystery, is watching when they are in danger—when looking through the clouds for an airport, when something breaks, and oil splashes over the windshield . . . But, also, sometimes He looks away. . . . One could say only that their dying young meant they would be remembered that way. Quietly, by myself, the tears came at last.

Lundquist was to have some problems, too, but not as serious, and not without a future. He finally reached England in his Spitfire, after several stops—one an engine failure over the Greenland ice cap, where, with full fuel tanks and no engine, he had to land, wheels up, on the cold, green ice.

When he reached Bascombe Down in England with a new engine and propeller, he, at last, got himself appointed to a British fighter combat squadron—against orders. However, he misread his wingman's signals, was shot down, and captured. He was taken to the Stalag III German camp for the rest of the war. After the war, he was to continue test flying, win the Thompson Trophy in the Cleveland Air Races, retire as a general, and become head of the Federal Aviation Administration.

I reported in over Newark and, in time, started our letdown to Mitchell, cutting back on the four engines and following Mitchell's landing instructions. On the final approach, Leach struggled into his proper seat for the landing. As we taxied in, I could see he was perspiring heavily. Other crew members who had been riding along crowded into the cockpit.

"How are you doing, sir?"

"Maybe we better get a wheelchair, or something."

"No, no. I'm okay. Just getting the flu. After we check in, I'll go hit the sack for a while. Be fine."

The solicitous crew members helped him down to the tarmac, and supported him as they walked up into the Mitchell Operations Office. I watched them and called softly, "Good luck. Thanks for the ride."

Then I picked up my suitcases and walked away from military flying in World War II. . . . I thought of the words of the English poet Laurence Binyon:

> They shall not grow old, as we that are left grow old:
> Age shall not weary them, nor the years condemn.
> At the going down of the sun and in the morning
> We will remember them.*

---

* "For the Fallen," *Collected Poems of Laurence Binyon*, Vol. 1, Bk. 4 [1914–1920] (London: Macmillan, 1931), 210.

EPILOGUE

To have our war service terminated before the war's end made us feel incomplete, that we had not been "in at the finish." After honing our skills and dedicating ourselves to the war effort, we were now surplus. And 38 WASPs had given their lives.

One hundred fifty WASPs signed on for nonflying duty in the Air Force. Two went to the Army, two to the Navy, and one to the RAF. Many of them remained in the service through the Vietnam War and most served as captains, majors, or lieutenant colonels, and many served overseas. Some took civilian jobs, when they could find them, ferrying civilian planes or instructing. A few ran flying schools, served on government flying safety boards, were control tower operators.

The WASPs were not the only women in war work to feel the new bias against them. The Rosie the Riveters, as the war began winding down, were suddenly no longer the heroines they once were. They were now standing in the way of returning soldiers, taking their jobs. Eleanor Roosevelt, Doris Kearns Goodwin points out, saw the dilemma, and asked, "But can we afford to deny women work?"

Because I had lost contact with the other WASPs while at Wright Field, I did not feel a part of them until much later. Actually, the WASP had always been a secret unsung group, and after disbandment they seemed to disperse and fade from the scene, until almost 20 years later when a WASP organization was formed. In 1977 the WASP were at last admitted to the Air Force by Congress, thanks to the help of Sen. Barry Goldwater and others and many active WASPs. Though it was too late for the G.I. Bill to help the WASP, they did find they could be buried in veterans' cemeteries!

It was not until the fiftieth anniversary of World War II, 1995–96, when new women military flyers were agitating for combat duty, that the WASPs were really discovered again and began to receive the interest and credit they deserved as pioneers. And because they had proved women could be professional military pilots then, today's military pilots were given a boost. Women pilots, in general, have increased in number about one-hundred-fold since World War II, but the question continues to come up: "Should women do this kind of flying, or that kind of flying?"

Today they confidently participate in every branch of aviation—air lines, testing, instructing, aeronautical engineering, and the ultimate, flying in space. Sally Ride was the first in space as a scientist, but Eileen Collins piloted the shuttle Discovery in 1996.

Although I understand Navy flyer Rosemary Conaster's ambition to "become a full professional in my chosen field," which to her and others means combat flying, I see a contradiction between women dedicated to the country and the future, and women dog-fighting, dropping bombs on villages, strafing foot soldiers. True, men do not relish these assignments either, but do we truly need women Amazons out to kill? If we are in danger of defeat, we might. But the argument is irrelevant. Women pilots in service with the Air Force or the Navy will, after all, be required to follow orders, whatever those orders are.

Though the WASP experience may well have been the most telling period in the lives of most of us, just as their war service is usually the favorite topic of men who served in war, it has had other profound effects. Having accomplished it, we developed courage and self-confidence for other challenges, personal ones and community or national ones. The women who were WASPs— and probably those who were WAACs and WAVES as well—have, besides their jobs, been leaders in their communities, have been honored in halls of fame, have spoken and written to educate young and old about aviation, public service, and the general joys and opportunities in flying.

Like a fair proportion of the disbanded WASPs, out of several possible futures I chose marriage—another all-encompassing job requiring dedication.

Bill Carl and I returned to NACA in Virginia to stay until V-J Day. I was no longer part of the test picture, though. In fact, morning sickness kept me pretty housebound. We saved up our gasoline for the weekends, which we spent with the Gilruths testing hydrofoils and rigid sails on Back River. Gilruth had a catamaran with hydrofoils and we had a small green runabout with the rigid sail. Jean Roché, designer of the first commercial lightplane, the Aeronca C-2, offered advice.

After the atomic bombs and V-J Day, in August 1945, we moved to Long Island, N.Y. We soon had two children (our daughter was ill for almost two years and required my constant attention). Bill was designing and building hydrofoil boats for the Navy, and soon he and Bob Gilruth (still at NACA) formed a company called Dynamic Developments, Inc. The first boat, painted orange for photographing test runs, had two air-cooled aircraft engines and three surface-piercing hydrofoils and went 92 MPH. This led to contracts for a 60-foot boat to go 60 knots, as well as outboard boats with foils. These we all drove at 35 MPH. Then Grumman Aerospace, seeing a good thing, bought out DDI, first buying 50 percent, then, later, the rest. But when NACA became NASA in 1958, Bill had to buy Gilruth's share of DDI to avoid conflict of interest with NASA contracts with Grumman. When a boat faster than the World War II PT boat was needed in Vietnam, both Grumman and Boeing were given contracts to build one. Both were tried out in Vietnam.

After John F. Kennedy was elected president in 1960 and issued his challenge to put a man on the moon, we rejoiced with Gilruth, then director of the Space Center in Houston, on the successes of Mercury, Gemini, and Apollo space shots, and met some of the astronauts. (Many WASPs, including me, had rather hoped to become astronauts. Though Jerry Cobb and others were given the tests, I'm afraid it was Gilruth who said no to risking women then.)

When astronauts Neil Armstrong and Buzz Aldrin on Apollo 11 were about to land on the moon in 1969, in the Grumman LEM landing module, we were on one of our sailing sorties in Ireland. While eating at a restaurant in Kinsale that night, we told the proprietor that we were associated with Grumman. He quickly motioned to us to follow him upstairs to watch on TV. As Armstrong started down the ladder to take his "small step for man," the proprietor suddenly turned off the TV and extracted the TV tube.

"It's not a good picture. I'll put in another tube." So we never saw the "big step for mankind."

In 1976, the National Air and Space Museum of the Smithsonian Institution opened. Somewhere between the Wright Brothers' plane and the space modules and rockets on the first floor was the Flight Testing Gallery. In it was our first jet-propelled plane, the XP-59A (the plain P-59 was a different plane entirely). A label panel with my picture commemorated the 1944 flight of the first woman to fly a jet (actually the YP-59A), plus the fact that Gen. Laurence Craigie was the first Air Force pilot to fly it. For years, I received interesting letters and requests for pictures and autographs from around the world. In 1995, the XP-59A was moved to the Milestones of Flight Gallery.

The next woman to fly a jet was Jacqueline Auriol of France in 1953, followed by Jackie Cochran. In Germany, Hanna Reitsch, a friend of Hitler's, flew a German rocket-propelled plane, the Me-163, though not a true turbo-jet, at Peenemunde in 1944.

In 1977, Bill retired from Grumman early. We sold our house, cars, and everything and set off in a dark-blue 45-foot ketch called *Audacious* for a two-year journey that included Bermuda, Canada, Nova Scotia, on to Ireland and England, through the French canals, up and down the Mediterranean as far as Turkey, and back across the Atlantic to the Caribbean, Bahamas, and home. Because of my WASP navigation skills, I was navigator, and often I called upon the same deity that appears to help pilots, when trying to find a harbor entrance to a new country, or something, anything, to reassure me we were on the right course. From all this came a book, *The Small World of Long-Distance Sailors*, published in 1985.

Both sailing and flying bring one into close contact with the earth. It's not hard to read its vital signs—the low production of fish with high production of pollution, the smoke and spread of cities, the rivers that have turned red or green or brown. Anthropologist Loren Eiseley, after viewing space photos of the earth, suggested that "the human race may be, after all, just a blight on the earth." Microbiologist René Dubos said, "We may be losing our humanness in the confusion of steel and concrete in the midst of noise, dirt and ugliness."

I, too, at this time became concerned about the state of the earth, and became a regular columnist on science and the environment for many publications (from *Newsday* to the *Bulletin of the Atomic Scientists*) and gave lectures and testified before Congress on vital environmental issues. Far from having a tame, sedentary life, I was chased on the road by angry dredgers, harassed by phone by wetlands destroyers, and when we fought a nuclear power plant in court the differential of my car was sawn through so the guts of the car fell on the road.

I took time as well to work with research doctors in a mental hospital, where I worked with patients on the wards and also made sketches during operations for paintings of surgical procedures doctors used for instruction and to illustrate published papers.

After the children were in school, I journeyed back to flying. Before I could instruct, I had to take a test. When my instructor signed off my log book, he was surprised to find that on the same page were recorded flights in the B-29 and the P-38. Among my students of all sizes and ages were United Air Lines third pilots who were there to get their instrument ratings. I did some flying for Dynamic Developments, Inc., too, ferrying personnel and engine parts.

In 1992, to celebrate 50 years of jet flight, General Craigie and I were invited to give a lecture on early jet flight at the National Air and Space Museum in Washington. Frank Whittle was in the audience. As part of our participation, we were invited to be photographed sitting in the cockpit of the museum's XP-59A. The cockpit felt familiar. It did not seem as long ago as 50 years! In the audience also were old friends (or should I say long-time friends) in the WASP. From that time, I have enjoyed taking part in WASP activities and renewing acquaintances. As the years go by, such friends—colleagues—become more significant.

In the Wright-Patterson Air Force Base Memorial Park there are two memorial statues of special interest. One remembers Flight Test pilots who lost their lives while stretching the boundaries of flight at Wright Field. The other, designed by WASP Dorothy Swain Lewis, remembers those WASPs who gave their lives in World War II and were also pioneers. In 1996, the WASP, as a group, was awarded the Milton Caniff Spirit of Flight Award by the National Aviation Hall of Fame in Dayton.

The spirit of flight will continue to inspire men and women to risk their lives and defy the elements to travel faster, farther, higher, in stealth and in space. The discovery of living cells on Mars will draw us into the mysteries of outer space. But in our concentration on hardware development, it would be wise to recall Charles Lindbergh's warning, in his foreword to Anne Lindbergh's *Listen! the Wind:* "The perfection of machinery tends to insulate man from contact with the elements in which he lives. The stratosphere planes of the future will cross the ocean without any sense of the water below."

Right now, as we approach the year 2000, the human outlook is somewhat bleak. Our concerns are with the bottom line, with money and power. The young want to escape reality with drugs. Computers isolate us in virtual realities. Only a few speak for the "elements in which we live." We live in confusion of what is right and what looks right. We must reintroduce ourselves to the elements if we want to improve our vision of the future. It is time to look out the window to get a sense of the water below.

APPENDIX A

Specifications for Aircraft Flown

SOURCES

The primary source was *Jane's Encyclopedia of Aviation* (New York: Crescent Books, 1995), but all specifications were cross-checked with the other sources.

Aviation History magazine.

A. Carl flight logs.

Chilstrom, Kenneth, and Perry Leary, eds. *Test Flying at Old Wright Field.* Omaha, Neb.: Westchester House, 1993.

Walker, Lois, and Shelby Wickam. *From Huffman's Prairie to the Moon: The History of Wright Patterson Air Force Base.* Washington, D.C.: U.S. Printing Office, 1980.

TRAINERS AND TRANSPORT

L-4 (Piper J-3)

Two-seater monoplane, fabric covered, wooden propeller, tailwheel. L = Liaison.

ENGINE: Standard model—Lycoming, Franklin, and Continental 65 hp, earlier models with 40- or 50-hp engines later model (Navy HE ambulance plane and USAF liaison plane with 130-hp Lycoming).

NUMBER MANUFACTURED: 14,125 (standard model)

L-5 (Stinson-Vultee)—Sentinel

Three-seater high-wing monoplane. Three versions: L-5, L-5A, and L-5B (L-5B carried stretcher or cargo).

ENGINE: 190-hp Lycoming 0-435-1

WING SPAN: 34.0 feet

LENGTH: 24.1 feet

MAXIMUM T/O WEIGHT: 2,158 pounds

MAXIMUM LEVEL SPEED: 120 MPH

NUMBER SUPPLIED TO USAF: 3,000

PT-19 (Fairchild)—Cornell
Tandem two-seater low-wing open cockpit monoplane (three versions). PT = Primary trainer.

ENGINE: 175-hp Ranger L-440-1

MAXIMUM SPEED: 130 MPH

WING SPAN: 36.0 feet

LENGTH: 27.11 feet

MAXIMUM T/O WEIGHT: 2,741 pounds

RANGE: 450 miles

NUMBER MANUFACTURED: 7,500

PT-13 (Stearman)—Kaydet
Tandem two-seater open cockpit biplane (also used by U.S. Navy, RAF, South America).

ENGINE: 220-hp Lycoming R-680-5

WING SPAN: 32.2 feet

LENGTH: 25.1 feet

MAXIMUM T/O WEIGHT: 2,717 pounds

MAXIMUM LEVEL SPEED: 124 MPH

RANGE: 4 hours 15 minutes

BT-13 (Vultee)—Valiant
Tandem two-seater, basic trainer metal monoplane with cockpit canopy. BT = Basic trainer.

ENGINE: 450 Pratt and Whitney R-985-AN-1, 3

MAXIMUM SPEED: 185 MPH

NUMBER MANUFACTURED: 11,537

AT-6 (North American)—Texan
Single-engine low-wing two-seater monoplane. AT = Advanced trainer. U.S. Navy designation: SNJ.

WING SPAN: 42 feet

LENGTH: 29 feet

HEIGHT: 11 feet 1 inch

ENGINE: 600-hp Pratt and Whitney R-1340

MAXIMUM SPEED: 210 MPH

CRUISING SPEED: 145 MPH

RANGE: 870 miles

SERVICE CEILING: 24,750 feet

NUMBER PRODUCED: 15,485

AT-17 (or UC-78) (Cessna)—Bobcat

Twin-engine wood and fabric four- to five-place advanced trainer.

ENGINES: Two 245-hp Jacobs R775-9 air-cooled radial engines

PROPELLERS: Hamilton Standard constant-speed or two-blade wooden fixed pitch

WING SPAN: 41 feet 11 inches

LENGTH: 32 feet 9 inches

MAXIMUM T/O WEIGHT: 5,700 pounds

MAXIMUM LEVEL SPEED: 195 MPH

RANGE: 750 miles

NUMBER PRODUCED: 3,323

AT-7, AT-10, AT-11 (Beechcraft) Kansan

Twin-engine advanced trainers for navigators and bombardiers. Nearly all of the 50,000 navigators and 45,000 bombardiers in World War II were trained in these aircraft.

AT-10: Four-seat monoplane, all wood, two 295-hp Lycoming engines.

AT-7 and AT-11: Model 18, all metal, using Wright, Jacobs, or Pratt and Whitney engines in several configurations, including gun turrets, bomb-bay doors and bomb racks, transparent nose, eight places.

C-45 (Beechcraft Model 18) (see above)

Twin-engine, all-metal, low-wing monoplane, all-purpose aircraft for eight persons. C = Cargo or transport. Used as cargo and personnel transport, ambulance, or for photography.

ENGINES: Two 450-hp Pratt & Whitney R985-AN-1,3

WING SPAN: 47 feet 8 inches

LENGTH: 34 feet 3 inches

MAXIMUM T/O WEIGHT: 7,850 pounds

MAXIMUM LEVEL SPEED: 215 MPH

RANGE: 700 miles

NUMBER SUPPLIED: 5,257 to allied forces in Canada, Britain and U.S.

C-47 (Douglas DC-3) "Gooney Bird" (RAF Dakota)

Twin-engine, low-wing monoplane transport aircraft with 21 seats plus crew. Designed in 1936 as a sleeper transport. In 1940, 10,000 transport version DC-3s were ordered by the AAF.

ENGINES: Wright Cyclone and Pratt & Whitney Wasp engines ranging from 1,000 to 1,200 hp

WING SPAN: 95.0 feet

LENGTH: 63 feet 9 inches

MAXIMUM T/O WEIGHT: 28,000 pounds

CRUISING SPEED: 170 MPH

RANGE: 1,025 miles

DC-3s are still flying. During the war they flew in forty countries and "flew more miles, hauled more freight, and carried more passengers than any other air craft in history."[1]

BOMBER AIRCRAFT

A-24A, A-24B (Douglas) Dauntless

Single-engine attack dive-bomber for pilot and gunner/observer. A = Attack bomber. U.S. Navy designation SBD-3. Used primarily in Pacific theater for all dive-bombing and scout duties and submarine patrols, 5,936 completed.

ENGINE: A-24A: 1,000-hp Wright R-1820-52 with two-speed superchargers. A-24B: 1,200-hp Wright R-1820-60.

WING SPAN: 41 feet 6 inches

LENGTH: 33 feet 1 inch

MAXIMUM T/O WEIGHT: 9,519 pounds

MAXIMUM LEVEL SPEED: 200–255 MPH

RANGE: 1,115 miles

ARMAMENT: Various—including one or two machine guns, one or two bombs (1,000 pounds), or depth charges

A-25, A-25A (Curtiss) Helldiver

Single-engine attack dive-bomber, two-seat, carrier borne. Navy version SB2C.

ENGINE: 1,700-hp Wright R-2600-8, with three-bladed Curtiss electric constant-speed propeller

WING SPAN: 49 feet 9 inches

LENGTH: 36 feet 8 inches

MAXIMUM T/O WEIGHT: 14,042 pounds

MAXIMUM LEVEL SPEED: 299+ MPH

RANGE: 1,925 miles

ARMAMENT: Four .50-caliber machine guns in wings, one in rear cockpit various versions, including seaplane model with cannon

NUMBER PRODUCED: 978 A-25s, 4,000 SB2Cs

B-25 (North American) Mitchell

Twin-engine versatile bomber with tricycle landing gear. B = Bomber. Served in every allied air force in both theaters. Jimmy Doolittle led a low-level raid over Tokyo with sixteen of these bombers.

ENGINES: B-25B: Two 1,700-hp Wright R-2600-9 Cyclone

WING SPAN: 67 feet 7 inches

LENGTH: 52 feet 11 inches

HEIGHT: 15 feet 9 inches

MAXIMUM T/O WEIGHT: 41,800 pounds

MAXIMUM LEVEL SPEED: 275–300 MPH, range 1,245 miles

ARMAMENT: Various, including machine guns forward, in side turrets, and tail, plus 3,000-pound bomb load in bomb bay. Armored, self-sealing fuel tanks

NUMBER PRODUCED: 9,816

B-26G (Martin) Marauder
Twin-engine bomber used in all theaters.
ENGINES: Two Pratt and Whitney 2,000-hp R-2800-43
WING SPAN: 71.0 feet (65.0 feet in earlier A and B models)
LENGTH: 58 feet 3 inches
MAXIMUM T/O WEIGHT: 38,200 pounds
MAXIMUM LEVEL SPEED: 287 MPH
RANGE: 1,200 miles (7 crew)
ARMAMENT: Twelve guns—in nose, side fuselage, dorsal turret, waist, ventral, and tail, 2,000-pound bomb load
NUMBER PRODUCED: 5,150

B-24 D-M (Consolidated) Liberator
Four-engine heavy bomber, wings high on the fuselage. Crew of ten. Used in all the-
    aters, especially on long-range missions to Ploesti oil refineries in Romania and to
    Benghazi in Libya.
ENGINES: Four 1,200-hp Pratt and Whitney R-1830-65 radial with turbochargers
WING SPAN: 110.0 feet
LENGTH: 67 feet 2 inches
HEIGHT: 15 feet 11 inches
MAXIMUM T/O WEIGHT: 64,500 pounds
MAXIMUM LEVEL SPEED: 300 MPH
COMBAT RANGE: 2,100 miles
ARMAMENT: Ten .50-caliber machine guns and 8,800 pounds of bombs in bomb bay
NUMBER PRODUCED: 18,800 (more than any other combat plane in World War II)

B-17E-G (Boeing) Flying Fortress
Four-engine heavy long-range bomber. Used in all theaters, especially in Guadalcanal,
    Africa, and Europe. 640,000 tons of bombs dropped over Germany in constant raids,
    and 6,660 planes shot down.
ENGINES: Four 1,600-hp Wright R-2600 Cyclone radial with superchargers
WING SPAN: 152.0 feet
LENGTH: 106.0 feet
MAXIMUM T/O WEIGHT: 84,000 pounds
MAXIMUM LEVEL SPEED: 199 MPH, Cruising speed: 184 MPH
RANGE: 5,200 miles
CEILING: 35,000 feet (except Wright Field Aero Med special plane with 43,000 feet)
NUMBER PRODUCED: 12,731

B-29A (Boeing) Superfortress
Four-engine heavy long-range bomber. Operational in Pacific theater. Gen. Curtis
    LeMay flew low-level raids over Japan and B-29s (*Enola Gay* and *Boch's Car*) deliv-
    ered atom bombs to Hiroshima and Nagasaki, respectively, August 6 and 9, 1945.
ENGINES: Four 2,200-hp Wright R-3350 radial

WING SPAN: 141 feet 3 inches

LENGTH: 99.0 feet

MAXIMUM T/O WEIGHT: 141,100 pounds

MAXIMUM LEVEL SPEED: 358 MPH

RANGE: 5,000 miles with maximum fuel load

ARMAMENT: 10–11 .50-caliber machine guns, one 20mm cannon, and 29,000 pounds of bombs

SPECIAL FEATURES: Pressurized cabin in three compartments, offensive and defensive radar, special wing aerofoil section to improve wing loading

FIGHTER AIRCRAFT
P-38 H-J (Lockheed) Lightning

Twin-engine long range versatile fighter and long range escort. P = Pursuit. Called "Forked tailed devil" by the Luftwaffe. "Credited with shooting down more Japanese planes than any other fighter in the Pacific."[2]

ENGINES: Two liquid-cooled 1,475-hp Allison V-1710-111/113, with superchargers and counter-rotating propellers

WING SPAN: 52.0 feet

LENGTH: 37 feet 10 inches

MAXIMUM T/O WEIGHT: 21,600 pounds

MAXIMUM LEVEL SPEED: 414 MPH

CRUISING SPEED: 290 MPH

RANGE: 450 miles (internal fuel only). Maximum range: 1,500 miles

ARMAMENT: Five machine guns and 1,600 underwing weapons and 20mm cannon

NUMBER MANUFACTURED: 9,923

"The P-38 was the only American fighter built before World War II to be still in production on V-J Day. The Lightning was used in all U.S. combat zones as a high- and low-altitude fighter, fighter escort, bomber, photo-reconnaissance aircraft, and low-level attack and rocket fighter, and smokescreen layer."[3]

P-40N (Curtiss) Warhawk (RAF Tomahawk)

Single-engine monoplane fighter. Served in all theaters with all Allied countries.

ENGINE: 1,360-hp liquid-cooled Allison V-17110-81

WING SPAN: 37 feet 4 inches

LENGTH: 33 feet 4 inches

MAXIMUM T/O WEIGHT: 8,850 pounds

MAXIMUM LEVEL SPEED: 362 MPH

CRUISING SPEED: 235 MPH

RANGE: 240 miles, 950 miles

SERVICE CEILING: 32,750 feet

ARMAMENT: Six .50-caliber machine guns, one 500-pound bomb

NUMBER PRODUCED: 13,738

P-47B, G, RP-47E (Republic) Thunderbolt "The Jug"

Largest and heaviest single-engine fighter. Served on all fronts as long-range escorts and as ground strafing fighter bombers. RP-47E—experimental P-47 with first fighter pressurized cabin.

ENGINE: 2,000-hp Pratt and Whitney R-2800 radial, air-cooled, turbosupercharger (P-47D: 2,535-hp, R-2800-59 WASP)

WING SPAN: 40 feet 9 inches

LENGTH: 36 feet 1 inch

MAXIMUM T/O WEIGHT: 19,400 pounds

MAXIMUM LEVEL SPEED: 428 MPH (One P-47D set speed record of 504 MPH.)

RANGE: 590 miles to 2,000 miles with extra fuel

ARMAMENT: Eight .50-caliber machine guns and two 1,000-pound bombs, 10 five-inch rockets

CEILING: 42,000 feet

NUMBER PRODUCED: 15,600

P-51B, D (North American) Mustang

Single-engine versatile fighter and long-range escort. Though the P-51 was first ordered by the British, it became the "pre-eminent long range escort fighter of World War II and in many respects the [U.S.'s] greatest all-around combat aircraft" ().[4] Among its advances were: laminar flow wing, wide-track landing gear, ducted coolant radiator under the rear fuselage. Some P-51s with extra fuel tanks behind the pilot seat were able to fly all the way to Berlin, although, until the tank was empty, the plane was unstable and difficult to fly. Other versions: A36A, F-6.

ENGINE: 1,520-hp Packard V-1650-3 (U.S. variant of Rolls Royce Merlin engine)

WING SPAN: 37.0 feet

LENGTH: 32 feet 3 inches

MAXIMUM T/O WEIGHT: 11,600 pounds

MAXIMUM LEVEL SPEED: 437 MPH

RANGE: 950–2,080 miles

CEILING: 31,350 feet

NUMBER PRODUCED: 15,586

ARMAMENT: Six .50-caliber machine guns, 10 five-inch rockets, 2,000-pound bomb load on wings

YP-59A (Bell) Airacomet

First U.S.-designed and -built turbojet fighter. Y = test evaluation model. Produced as a fighter, rather than a mere experimental craft, the Airacomet proved directionally unstable for a gun platform, though it reached speed and altitude goals. Nevertheless, it was the pioneer in demonstrating that this entirely new propulsion by turbo jet was practical and possible.

ENGINES: Two gas-turbine jet engines, General Electric type I-A, developed from the British Whittle jet engine

WING SPAN: 45 feet 6 inches

LENGTH: 38 feet 2 inches
HEIGHT: 12 feet
WEIGHT: 9,000 pounds
MAXIMUM T/O WEIGHT: 13,700 pounds
MAXIMUM LEVEL SPEED: 414 MPH (with I-A-16 engines)
CEILING: 47,600 feet (U.S. altitude record for single-place fighter, 12-15-1943)
MAXIMUM POUNDS OF THRUST: 1,650 pounds at 16,500 rpm
ARMAMENT: One 37mm cannon, three .50-caliber machine guns, bomb racks on wings
NUMBER PRODUCED: Three XP-59A, 13 YP-59A, 20+ production P-59

FOREIGN AIRCRAFT
Avro 683 Lancaster
Heavy British bomber.
ENGINES: Four 1,280-hp Rolls Royce MerlinsMAXIMUM LEVEL SPEED: 275 MPH
RANGE: 1,660 miles
ARMAMENT: 10 machine guns, 14,000-pound bomb load

De Havilland Mosquito
British twin-engine wooden light bomber.
ENGINES: Two 1,710-hp Merlins
MAXIMUM LEVEL SPEED: 425 MPH
RANGE: 3,500 miles, various versions

Supermarine Spitfire
British fighter.
ENGINE: One 2,050-hp Rolls Royce Griffon
MAXIMUM LEVEL SPEED: 448 MPH
RANGE: 850 miles
ARMAMENT: Cannon, machine guns, bombs

Junkers Ju-88
German bomber.
ENGINES: Two 1,340-hp Jumo 211J
MAXIMUM SPEED: 292 MPH

C-64, Nordyne Norseman
Canadian transport.
ENGINE: One 550-hp Pratt and Whitney R-1340-AN
MAXIMUM T/O WEIGHT: 7,400 pounds
CRUISING SPEED: 141 MPH
RANGE: 464 miles

CIVILIAN AIRCRAFT
Stinson Reliant
Five-seat commercial high-wing monoplane (as British AT-19, three-seat navigation
    trainer).
ENGINE: One 290-hp Lycoming
MAXIMUM LEVEL SPEED: 141 MPH

Beechcraft Staggerwing
Four-seat biplane.
ENGINE: One 450-hp Pratt and Whitney Wasp Junior MAXIMUM LEVEL SPEED: 198 MPH

Beechcraft Bonanza
V-tailed, five-seat, low-wing monoplane.
ENGINE: 285-hp Continental Engine IO 520 BA
MAXIMUM LEVEL SPEED: 209 MPH
Aircraft flown after the war not listed.

OTHER AIRCRAFT MENTIONED IN TEXT BUT NOT FLOWN

XP-80 (Lockheed) Shooting Star
Low-wing cantilever monoplane with a knife-edge laminar flow wing section. First jet
    fighter to become operational (as F-80) but too late for World War II.
ENGINE: Allison J-33-A-23, 4,000 pounds thrust, turbo jet
WING SPAN: 39 feet 11 inches
LENGTH: 34 feet 6 inches
MAXIMUM T/O WEIGHT: 16,856 pounds
MAXIMUM LEVEL SPEED: 580 MPH
CRUISING SPEED: 439 MPH
RANGE: 1,380 miles
ARMAMENT: Six .50-caliber machine guns, rockets, bombs and napalm bombs

XP-82 (North American) Twin Mustang
Two P-51 airframes wedded at the wing to form a twin engine, twin tail, twin cockpit
    airplane. Designed for long-range escort duty, it was the fastest propeller-driven
    fighter, with the longest range. It served mainly in Korea.
ENGINES: Two 1,380-hp Packard (Merlin) V-1, 650s
WING SPAN: 51 feet 3 inches
MAXIMUM WEIGHT: 24,600 pounds
MAXIMUM LEVEL SPEED: 482 MPH
RANGE: 2,200 miles
CEILING: 39,000 feet
ARMAMENT: Six .50-caliber guns, 25 five-inch rockets, 4,000 pounds of bombs

P-39 (Bell) Airacobra
Single-engine fighter which served in all World War II theaters.
ENGINE: 1,200-hp Allison liquid-cooled V-1710-85
WING SPAN: 34.0 feet
LENGTH: 30 feet 2 inches
MAXIMUM T/O WEIGHT: 8,300 pounds
MAXIMUM LEVEL SPEED: 385 MPH
RANGE: 675 miles
ARMAMENT: 37mm cannon in nose, four .50-caliber machine guns, one 500-pound bomb

XB-49 (Northrop) Flying Wing
Two eight-jet prototypes, one of which crashed during testing.

NOTES

1. Lois Walker and Shelby Wickam, *From Huffman's Prairie to the Moon: The History of Wright Patterson Air Force Base* (Washington, D.C.: U.S. Printing Office, 1980), 239.
2. Ibid., 245.
3. *Jane's Encyclopedia of Aviation* (New York: Crescent Books, 1995), 600.
4. *Jane's*, 708.

APPENDIX B

Costs of Representative Aircraft, WWII

Airplane	Cost[a]
Heavy bombers	
B-29	$509,465
B-17	187,742
B-24	215,516
Medium bombers	
B-25	$116,752
B-26	192,427
Fighters	
P-38	$ 97,147
P-39	50,666
P-40	44,892
P-47	83,001
P-51	50,985
P-59	123,477
Transports	
C-45	$ 48,830
C-47	85,035

Source: Lois Walker and Shelby Wickam, *From Huffman's Prairie to the Moon: The History of Wright Patterson Air Force Base* (Washington, D.C.: U.S. Printing Office, 1980), 235.

[a]In 1944 dollars.

Note: Jet fighters of the 1990s cost in the $50,000,000 range.

REFERENCES

Air and Space Magazine.

Aviation History Magazine.

Biddle, Wayne. *Barons of the Sky.* New York: Simon and Schuster, 1991.

Carpenter, David M. *Flame Powered.* Lynn, Mass.: General Electric, 1992.

Chilstrom, Kenneth, and Perry Leary, eds. *Test Flying at Old Wright Field.* Omaha, Neb.: Westchester House, 1993.

Douglas, Deborah. "United States Women in Aviation, 1940–1985." Washington, D.C.: Smithsonian Institution Press, 1990.

Dubos, René. *So Human an Animal.* New York: Scribner's, 1968.

Eiseley, Loren. *The Immense Journey.* New York: Vintage Books, 1946.

Goodwin, Doris Kearns. *No Ordinary Time.* New York: Simon and Schuster, 1994.

Granger, Byrd Howell. *On Final Approach.* Scottsdale, Ariz.: Falconer Publications, 1991.

Grun, Bernard. *The Timetables of History.* 3rd ed. New York: Simon and Schuster, 1991.

Heiman, Grover. *Jet Pioneers.* New York: Duell Sloan and Pierce, 1963.

Jane's Encyclopedia of Aviation. New York: Crescent Books, 1995.

Keil, Sally Van Wagenen. *Those Wonderful Women in Their Flying Machines.* New York: Rawson Wade, 1979.

Lindbergh, Anne Morrow. *Listen! the Wind.* New York: Harcourt Brace, 1938.

Shute, Nevil. *Slide Rule.* New York: Ballantine Books, 1972.

Stevenson, William. *A Man Called Intrepid.* New York: Ballantine Books, 1976.

Walker, Lois, and Shelby Wickam. *From Huffman's Prairie to the Moon: The History of Wright Patterson Air Force Base.* Washington, D.C.: U.S. Printing Office, 1980.

INDEX